The Big Book of Primary Club Resources: Science and Outdoor Learning

Fe Luton and Lian Jacobs

Routledge
Taylor & Francis Group

LONDON AND NEW YORK

First published 2019
by Routledge
2 Park Square, Milton Park, Abingdon, Oxon OX14 4RN

and by Routledge
52 Vanderbilt Avenue, New York, NY 10017

Routledge is an imprint of the Taylor & Francis Group, an informa business

British Library Cataloguing-in-Publication Data
A catalogue record for this book is available from the British Library

Library of Congress Cataloging-in-Publication Data
A catalog record for this book has been requested

ISBN: 978-1-138-31890-8 (hbk)
ISBN: 978-1-138-31896-0 (pbk)
ISBN: 978-0-429-45418-9 (ebk)

Typeset in Helvetica
by Apex CoVantage, LLC

Printed and bound by CPI Group (UK) Ltd, Croydon, CR0 4YY

For Otis, Esther, Tilly and Rory

Contents

Contributors

Fe Luton

Fe has over 20 years' experience working in the education sector as a teacher, Early Years and Key Stage 1 manager, museum education officer, governor, researcher, writer and trainer. She has been writing and developing teacher resources for many years, and has written for the TES, Scholastic and The Hamilton Trust. Fe has previously run arts clubs, maths clubs, eco-clubs and sports clubs across the primary phase.

Lian Jacobs

Lian has over 17 years' experience working in the education sector. She has had a successful and long teaching career across Key Stage 2, during which time she has worked as a Senior Teacher, Leading Literacy Teacher and Advanced Skills Teacher. She has experience in mentoring and coaching both NQTs and teachers working in schools that require improvement. Lian has run an array of clubs in schools, including: singing, art, board games, gardening and cookery.

Introduction

The Big Book of Primary Club Resources book series aims to take the strain out of club planning by providing inspiring, well-planned activities that are easy to resource, set up and run, with children from ages 4–11.

Running a science and outdoor learning club

Science and outdoor learning clubs can be enormous fun and hugely rewarding for both teacher and children. Unfortunately, they can also become very time-consuming, with significant amounts of preparation and clearing-up required. As a teacher, you may also find yourself naturally drawn to things you have covered in your science lessons, especially if you don't have a science background.

Here we offer quick, easily prepared activities that focus on aspects of science that complement but are not always explicitly taught in the National Curriculum. The plans build week-on-week, developing skills, piquing interest and even introducing many science and outdoor explorations that children can easily continue to explore at home.

With activity suggestions for three age groups (4–7 years; 7–9 years and 9–11 years), the club can be suitable for whichever age group best fits your needs.

Where appropriate, we include suggestions for ways to share the preparation load with the children, by encouraging them to gather resources or brainstorm ideas outside of club time.

All club sessions can be run in as little as 30 minutes, or expanded to last an hour.

Navigating this book

This book contains twelve blocks, each broken down into six sessions. While it is useful to complete whole blocks at a time, the sessions are generally designed so that you can dip in and out. The blocks can also be completed in any order you wish. Some of the outdoor and nature blocks have a seasonal focus, so you may wish to run these in the autumn or summer terms.

At the beginning of every block there is a session-overview, and a broad outline of the preparation required for each.

You may wish to have internet access for some of the sessions, to share ideas and to look at how some of the experiments work, although this is not a pre-requisite.

Beyond the specific resources listed for each session, it will be helpful to have access to basic scientific equipment as well as an outdoor nature space. Some blocks, such as 'Magnetic and Electrical Wonders,' will require specialist equipment to complete.

We recommend that any resources you use such as magazines or newspapers should always be checked for inappropriate content. Always consider the health and safety issues of each session – those with very specific hazards are highlighted in the 'helpful hints' section of the activity.

1   Art and nature

Over the course of this block, children will use nature to create and inspire pieces of artwork. The block can be completed at any time of the year, although autumn, spring and summer will offer a wider choice of colour and texture to explore.

This block includes the following sessions (key resources underneath):

1 **Natural paints**
   Mixing bowls; spoons; pebbles; water; pigments: e.g. turmeric, paprika, instant coffee, charcoal, cooked beetroot, blueberries, blackberries; paint pots; thin strips of card; paintbrushes; cellophane
2 **Landscape painting**
   Sample landscape images; paints from Session one; paintbrushes; painting paper; clipboards or painting boards; drawing pencils; mixing trays
3 **Outdoor photography**
   Digital cameras; printer; mounting paper
4 **Nature's textures**
   Nature items; aluminium foil; A4 card; PVA glue
5 **Anthony Goldsworthy: artist study**
   Examples of Goldsworthy art online (www.goldsworthy.cc.gla.ac.uk/); digital camera; chalk; paint
6 **Collaborative tree sculpture**
   Decorative items: bottles, CDs, metal and plastic scraps, fabric, nature items; wool, ribbons and string; glue sticks and PVA glue; wire

In preparation for this block, gather together the ingredients for creating natural paints and look for examples of nature-inspired art. You will also need access to an outdoor area with trees and plants to create the artwork in Sessions two through six.

Session one
Natural paints

Paint is a mainstay in most creative spaces, but how were pigments created in the days before poster paints? Children will spend this session creating their own homemade, plant-based paints that they will then use in Session two to paint an outdoor landscape.

Resources needed

Mixing bowls; spoons; pebbles; water; pigments: e.g. turmeric, paprika, instant coffee, charcoal, cooked beetroot, blueberries, blackberries; paint pots; thin strips of card; paintbrushes; cellophane

Activity

1   Ask children how they think paint is made. Explain that it contains a range of ingredients, depending on the type of paint. Paint is generally created using pigments, resin, solvent and additives. The pigments often come from metals (oxides) or other natural substances (see Figure 1.1)
2   Explain that today, children are going to create their own paints using plant sources for their pigments (see Figures 1.2–1.5)
3   Show children the paint pigments (turmeric, paprika, instant coffee, charcoal, cooked beetroot, blueberries and blackberries) and ask them to suggest how they think they might create paint from these items. Give them a couple of minutes to discuss in pairs. Then explain that the paints will be made by crushing or squashing pigment in their bowls using the pebbles, adding water if required. Highlight that children may need to use more than one pigment to create the colour they are after
4   Working in pairs, children then go about making two or three colours (make sure each pair makes different colours to ensure that a range of colours are created within the group). They will need to make enough paint to be shared with everyone for landscape painting in the next session
5   Once finished, children paint some sample strips to glue around the paint pots they are to be stored in, so that children can see the colour of the dried paint. Cover each paint pot with cellophane to store

4–7 years – children make the colour as described

7–9 years – children make different shades of the same colour

9–11 years – children make versions of the same colour, e.g. brighter, deeper, redder

Key questions

- How could you make the colour brighter/different?
- How do you think the paint will look on paper? Will it dry the same colour?

Helpful hints

- If the paint becomes too runny, add some honey to thicken it up

Figure 1.1 Paint pigments

Figure 1.2 Berries

Figure 1.3 Beetroot

Figure 1.4 Charcoal

Figure 1.5 Coffee

Prep for next session (landscape painting)

Store the paints for next session. Children may like to make more paints at home to bring in

Session two
Landscape painting

Having created their own all-natural, plant-based paints during Session one, this week children are going to test out their products as they use them to paint a landscape.

Resources needed

Sample landscape images; paints from Session one; paintbrushes; painting paper; clipboards or painting boards; drawing pencils; mixing trays

Activity

1 Look at the landscape images and ask children to identify ones they like and why. Highlight the range of subjects and variety of colours involved. Then show children Figures 1.6–1.8, highlighting the order in which the landscapes have been painted (sketch lines first for the main sections, background painted, detail painted)
2 Explain that children will paint their own landscape today using the paints they made in Session one. Do children think the paint might feel different to poster paints, acrylics, oils or watercolours? What was the liquid ingredient? Water! So these paints will be a bit like watercolours. They may also be a bit textured
3 Give children paper and a clipboard and head to an outdoor area where they can paint a landscape. It doesn't matter if it is a built-up landscape. The main criteria are that children have space to paint and that they can subdivide what they see into broad sections
4 Children sketch then paint their landscapes, sharing the paints from Session one

   4–7 years – children use the paints as they are. They paint clear sections and include some detail

   7–9 years – children mix some of the paints to make shades. They paint clear sections and include detail

   9–11 years – children mix some of the paints to create new colours. They paint clear sections and include detail and an element of perspective

Key questions

● How will you divide your view into broad sections?
● Which colours could you mix to create a new colour?

Helpful hints

● Emphasise that children don't have to include every detail they see in a landscape painting
● If you don't have outdoor access, children can paint landscapes from photos

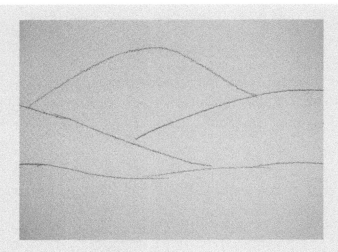

Figure 1.6 Sketch the main sections

Figure 1.7 Paint the background

Figure 1.8 Add details

Prep for next session (outdoor photography)

Ask children to have a go at taking some nature photographs and to bring them in to share. Make sure you have access to digital cameras

Session three
Outdoor photography

Nature is full of colour, shape, texture and form, which makes it ripe for interesting and beautiful photography. Children are going to try out some artistic manoeuvres this week, and will be finding ways to take creative images of their immediate natural environment.

Resources needed

Digital cameras; printer; mounting paper

Activity

1 Show children Figures 1.9–1.14 and look at the images that they have hopefully brought in. Ask them to suggest two words for each photo that they feel describe it, or reflect how it makes them feel
2 Which photography techniques have been used in the photographs? Note that some are close-up, zoomed-in, or only include part of an object; others include a wide array of features; some are taken from interesting angles; some are black and white, while others are bursting with vibrant colours. All of these photography techniques help to create interesting, artistic images
3 Explain that children are going to head outside with a digital camera and, in pairs, look for interesting natural features to photograph. They should identify what they are going to take a picture of and the technique they will use
4 Once children have taken at least 10–15 photographs they are happy with, they should come back inside and select their best three photographs for printing. Once they are printed, children can mount their photographs for exhibition

4–7 years – children take highly zoomed photographs that isolate a texture or colour. They also take photographs that show an entire item (a tree or plant, for example)

7–9 years – children take highly zoomed photographs that isolate a texture or colour. They also take photographs that show an entire item (a tree or plant, for example), as well as photographs that show part of an item (a branch or flower, for example). They consider how light hits the object they are photographing

9–11 years – children take highly zoomed photographs that isolate a texture or colour. They also take photographs that show an entire item (a tree or plant, for example), as well as photographs that show part of an item (a branch or flower, for example). They consider how light hits the object they are photographing and experiment with black and white photographs and other filters available on the cameras they are using

Key questions

● How would you describe the photograph?
● How does the light hit the object you are photographing?

Helpful hints

● If children zoom in too far and can't focus, get them to zoom back out again and retry

Figure 1.9 Zoomed-in

Figure 1.10 Close-up

Figure 1.11 Wider image

Figure 1.12 Interesting angle

Figure 1.13 Black and white

Figure 1.14 Vibrant colours

Prep for next session (nature's textures)

Ask children to find some nature items that have various textures (e.g. leaves, bark)

Session four
Nature's textures

Having explored texture through photography in Session three, children are going to get a more hands-on experience during this session as they create metallic 'rubbings' to incorporate into a piece of abstract art.

Resources needed

Nature items; aluminium foil; A4 card; PVA glue

Activity

1   Have a look at the nature items you have collected and that hopefully children have brought in. Get them to pick one up and describe to a partner how it feels. Children then group items according to these descriptions. For example, they might have a group of bumpy items, a group of spikey items and a group of ridged items
2   Explain that children are going to explore texture by creating foil 'rubbings' of the surface of a selection of items. Show them how to do this using a leaf or shell. Place the foil carefully over the item and use cotton wool to rub gently over the foil until the texture of the item has become embedded onto it. Remove the foil and gently open it out (see Figure 1.15)
3   Explain that children will collect a range of interesting textures using this technique, then they will create a collaged piece of abstract art by trimming, arranging and sticking down the segments of foil onto card (see Figure 1.16)
4   Set children to work on their rubbings and collage. When it comes to the latter, note that the foil should not be flattened onto the card, but glued using PVA glue on the sections that can most easily be stuck down

4–7 years – children find strong textures to use. They collect three or four foils for their art

7–9 years – children find a range of textures to use, including subtle ones. They collect six or seven foils for their art

9–11 years – children find a range of textures to use, including subtle ones. They collect at least ten foils for their art

Key questions

● How would you describe the textures?
● How have you decided to arrange the foils?

Helpful hints

● If children want to create a foil rubbing for a very spikey item, they will need to be extra gentle so as not to break the foil

Figure 1.15 Create foil rubbings

Figure 1.16 Foil rubbing collage

Prep for next session (Anthony Goldsworthy: artist study)

Challenge children to find out about Anthony Goldsworthy

Session five
Anthony Goldsworthy: artist study

Today, children are going to meet the king of nature art: Anthony Goldsworthy. Goldsworthy is a British artist who uses nature as a medium. He creates his artwork in the great outdoors, using items gathered locally, before photographing the finished pieces. Children will be creating their own nature sculpture today as they explore colour, form, texture and shape in nature.

Resources needed

Examples of Goldsworthy art online (www.goldsworthy.cc.gla.ac.uk/); digital camera; chalk; paint

Activity

1   Show children examples of Anthony Goldsworthy's art and ask them to identify the materials used. Do they like his nature sculptures? Ask them to describe some of them and note the colours, shapes and textures
2   Take children outside to collect a range of natural items with interesting colours, shapes and textures
3   Get children into small groups and ask them to put all of their found items together and group them by colour, form, shape or texture
4   Children then create their own nature sculptures similar to those in Figures 1.17–1.19 that have a focus on shape, form, texture or colour. They can use chalk or paints to add embellishments, then photograph the end result

    4–7 years – children group general colours, shapes and textures. They create lines, circles or swirls with their items

    7–9 years – children group colours, shapes and textures in interesting ways. They create more complex line configurations, circles or swirls with their items. Children use language to describe the textures

    9–11 years – children focus on changing colour shades in small increments and they group shapes. They create complex line configurations, circles, swirls and shapes with their items. Children use advanced language to describe texture and articulate artistic reasons for the form and structure of their sculpture

Key questions

● Can you describe the textures, shades, colours and shapes?
● How do the items complement each other?

Helpful hints

● Encourage children to collect more items than they think they will need, ensuring they have the widest possible range of options when it comes to creating their sculpture

Figure 1.17 Leaf sculpture

Figure 1.18 Rock sculpture

Figure 1.19 Conker and twig sculpture

Prep for next session (collaborative tree sculpture)

Ask children to bring in wool, old CDs and small used water bottles

Session six
Collaborative tree sculpture

To round off this block on nature art, children are going to pay homage to the mighty tree and create a collaborative dressed tree sculpture. They will create decorations which can then be secured to a favourite local tree.

Resources needed

Decorative items: bottles, CDs, metal and plastic scraps, fabric, nature items, wool, ribbons and string; glue sticks and PVA glue; wire

Activity

1 Take a look at the dressed tree in Figure 1.20. What has been used to decorate it? Explain that tree dressing is an ancient tradition that celebrates trees and our relationship with them. Linking art with nature, tree dressing highlights the value attached to nature

2 In groups, children come up with some ideas for decorative items. These should fit in with nature but also add elements that reflect light and incorporate colour and texture. Children explore the materials and items available in order to come up with ideas (see Figures 1.21 and 1.22 for examples). Allocate to each group a natural colour (sky blue, grass green, daffodil yellow, rose red, etc.), and explain that this colour needs to feature in some way in all their decorations

3 Children create their decorations, and then everyone goes out to dress the chosen tree. This is a collaborative form of sculpture, so children need to decide among themselves how the decorations will be hung. Use wire or string to attach decorations. Children also tie and hang ribbons on the tree

   4–7 years – children create abstract decorations

   7–9 years – children create layered decorations. They include some items that will glint in the light

   9–11 years – children create layered decorations with a range of textures and shades. They make decorations that will glint in the light

Key questions

● How will your decoration look in the tree?
● How will light interact with your decoration?
● How will you use ribbon to decorate the tree?

Helpful hints

● Have a low stepladder available to help decorate higher branches
● Try not to use paper and card, as these will start to disintegrate at the first sign of rain

Figure 1.20 Tree dressed with ribbons

Figure 1.21 Tree decoration

Figure 1.22 Tree decoration

Prep for next session

Have a look through and decide which topic you will do next time – the introduction page of each chapter will tell you what you need to prep

2 Special effects science

Over the course of this block, children will explore some sensational chemistry and tricks of the special effects trade. They will create concoctions, cause reactions and explore visual effects with mirrors and lighting.

This block includes the following sessions (key resources underneath):

1 **Erupting volcanoes**
   Goggles; trays; bicarbonate of soda; white vinegar; washing-up liquid; red food colouring; small plastic water bottles; lemons; knives
2 **Invisible ink**
   Example of hidden message written in lemon juice: perhaps 'can you make your own invisible ink?'; cotton buds; paper; 'inks' to try: lemon juice, milk, vinegar, honey, petroleum jelly, white crayons; highlighter pens; water; torch or table lamps
3 **Fake blood and wounds**
   Modelling clay or air-drying clay; blood ingredients: cornflour, icing sugar, instant coffee granules, gravy granules, golden syrup, washing-up liquid, red food colouring, red powder paint; mixing bowls; kettle
4 **Slimy substances**
   Slime/snot ingredients: PVA glue, water, bicarbonate of soda, contact lens saline, food colourings, including green; Oobleck ingredients: cornflour, water (cold); mixing bowls
5 **Light fantastic**
   Prisms; small mirrors; water; bowls; paper; torches; coloured tissue paper; coloured acetate gels or film; black card; glue sticks
6 **Disco magic**
   Mirrors; pens; paper; polystyrene balls; modelling clay; wooden skewers; glitter; CDs cut into small pieces; drawing pins; shiny paper or card cut into small pieces; PVA glue; torches

In preparation for this block, consider any risks that may need to be assessed when mixing substances together, such as eye and skin protection, as well as ensuring that children don't eat their mixtures. Also, make sure that you have read through the 'helpful hints,' which explain some of the science behind the activities. You will also need a range of household ingredients for the first four sessions, which may be worth sourcing well in advance.

Session one
Erupting volcanoes

We are starting off this block with a bang. Well, at least with an eruption. Children will build a model volcano and investigate the reaction between various quantities of bicarbonate of soda and vinegar, to see who can create the most impressive eruption.

Resources needed

Goggles; trays; bicarbonate of soda; white vinegar; washing-up liquid; red food colouring; small plastic water bottles; lemons; knives

Activity

1 Show children the 'ingredients' for today's special effect (bicarbonate of soda and vinegar). Note what they are and ask what children think might happen if they are mixed together. Give children a pot of vinegar and get then to put a pinch of the bicarbonate of soda into the pot, observing what happens. There should be a fizz. Note that these substances are called reactants because they react with each other. Ask children what they think might happen if the substances were used in larger quantities

2 Explain that children are going to have a go at creating an erupting volcano by mixing these reactants in given quantities. After this, they can test out different quantities of each ingredient to see if they can create an even larger reaction. But first children need to make their volcano. In pairs, children use modelling clay to create a hollow volcano-shaped mound that a small disposable water bottle can fit into (see Figure 2.1). These should be placed on trays, ready to erupt

3 Children put on goggles, then put two teaspoons of bicarbonate of soda, a squirt of washing liquid, and a few drops of red food colouring into their water bottle. They put the bottle into their volcano, add 50 ml of white vinegar, stand back and watch. Children record their eruptions to create a movie version of an erupting volcano

4 Children then make a lemon volcano (see Figure 2.2). Cut the top off a lemon, squeeze out the juice and pith. Add the juice back in, followed by bicarbonate of soda

4–7 years – children follow the guidance and make simple observations

7–9 years – children follow the guidance for both types of volcano. They make observations and offer their thoughts on what has happened

9–11 years – children experiment with the given ingredients to come up with their own eruption recipe proportions. They make observations and use scientific language to explain what is happening

Key questions

● What happens when the substances are mixed? What do you think is in the bubbles?
● What happens if you change the ratio of bicarbonate of soda to vinegar?

Helpful hints

● Note: when the bicarbonate of soda (a base) is mixed with the vinegar (an acid), carbon dioxide is released. It is this carbon dioxide which causes the fizzing

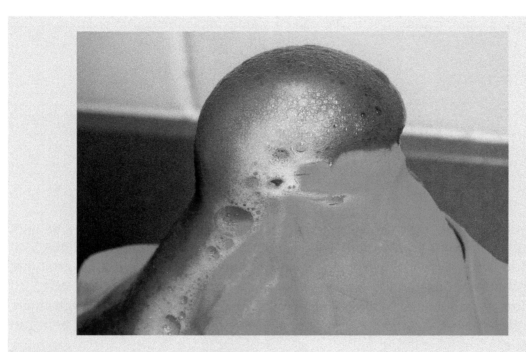

Figure 2.1 Clay and bottle volcano

Figure 2.2 Lemon volcano

Prep for next session (invisible ink)

Make a hidden message out of lemon juice to show children at the beginning of Session two

Session two
Invisible ink

Espionage is the name of the game this week, as children experiment with creating messages using invisible ink, trying out a range of possible 'inks' and working out what needs to be done to make them reveal their secrets.

Resources needed

Example of a hidden message written in lemon juice: perhaps 'can you make your own invisible ink?'; cotton buds; paper; 'inks' to try: lemon juice, milk, vinegar, honey, petroleum jelly, white crayons; highlighter pens; water; torch or table lamps

Activity

1 Show children your invisible message – can they read what you've written? Explain that there is a hidden message on the paper that needs to be revealed. Shine a torch or lamp close to the page until the message appears. Explain that children are going to try out various substances today to see if they can make a good invisible ink

2 Ask them what the key property is of any invisible ink. Clarify that it needs to be invisible! Children work in small groups. Give them the ingredients (see Figures 2.3–2.8) and challenge them to try writing messages with each one, using cotton buds to write with. Any substances that don't appear invisible on the paper should be disregarded immediately

3 Children then try to reveal their messages using the highlighter pens, water, torches or a table lamp. Note that it is the heat of the light source that reveals those messages that respond to light. Children should discuss what is happening and why

4 In their groups, children decide which of the substances makes the best invisible ink, then write messages for other groups to try to reveal!

4–7 years – children test out three substances, including crayons. They offer observations

7–9 years – children test out four substances, including crayons and petroleum jelly. They offer observations and attempt to make connections between the substance and how it is revealed

9–11 years – children test out five or six substances, including crayons and petroleum jelly. They offer scientific explanations for what they observe

Key questions

● What is happening to reveal the message?
● Do you think a reaction is taking place?

Helpful hints

● Note: the heat of the lamp or torch causes a chemical reaction with the lemon juice, vinegar and milk to reveal the message
● If the petroleum jelly messages do not appear, try to make the room very dark – they should glow

Figure 2.3 Lemon

Figure 2.4 Milk

Figure 2.5 Vinegar

Figure 2.6 Honey

Figure 2.7 Petroleum jelly

Figure 2.8 White crayons

Prep for next session (fake blood and wounds)

Mix up a couple of examples of next session's blood mixtures to show children

Session three
Fake blood and wounds

This week it's going to get gory, as children explore the world of prosthetics, attempt to make a realistic wound using clay and create fake blood. Children will explore the properties of substances when mixed with hot or cold water, and how they behave when they interact with other substances – lots of opportunities for predicting and observing.

Resources needed

Modelling or air-drying clay; card squares; blood ingredients: cornflour, icing sugar, instant coffee granules, gravy granules, golden syrup, washing-up liquid, red food colouring, red powder paint; mixing bowls; kettle

Activity

1   Show children Figure 2.9 and ask them if they think it is real. Explain that it is a prosthetic wound – a form of makeup whereby materials like latex are glued to an actor's skin. The aim is to make it look like people have been injured
2   Explain that today children are going to make their own prosthetic wounds and create some fake blood. Show children how to create a wound using modelling or air-drying clay (see Figure 2.10). They put this on a square of card before making some blood
3   Challenge children to experiment with various ingredients to create a liquid similar in colour and consistency to blood. It should be gloopy, a bit sticky and a deep dark red colour. They will need a thickener: cornflour, icing sugar or golden syrup; a colourant: gravy granules, instant coffee granules, red powder paint or red food colouring; and a liquid: washing-up liquid or water
4   Children then add their 'blood' to their prosthetic wound and take a photograph

4–7 years – children first try mixing icing sugar, water, food colouring, and coffee granules (in a paste with hot water); then golden syrup, washing-up liquid and red powder paint paste. They make observations about how the substances mix together

7–9 years – children have a go at selecting their own ingredients, then if unsuccessful they try the blood mixtures for 4- to 7-year-olds. They make observations about how the substances mix together, offering reasons for what they see

9–11 years – children select their own ingredients. If unsuccessful after several attempts, they try the blood mixtures in 4- to 7-year-olds. They make observations about how the substances mix together, using scientific language and offering reasons for what they see

Key questions

● What happens when you mix these substances together?
● How has the consistency of the mixture changed?

Helpful hints

- Make sure you have risk assessed the use of hot water
- Note: cornflour behaves differently when mixed with hot or cold water – try it out

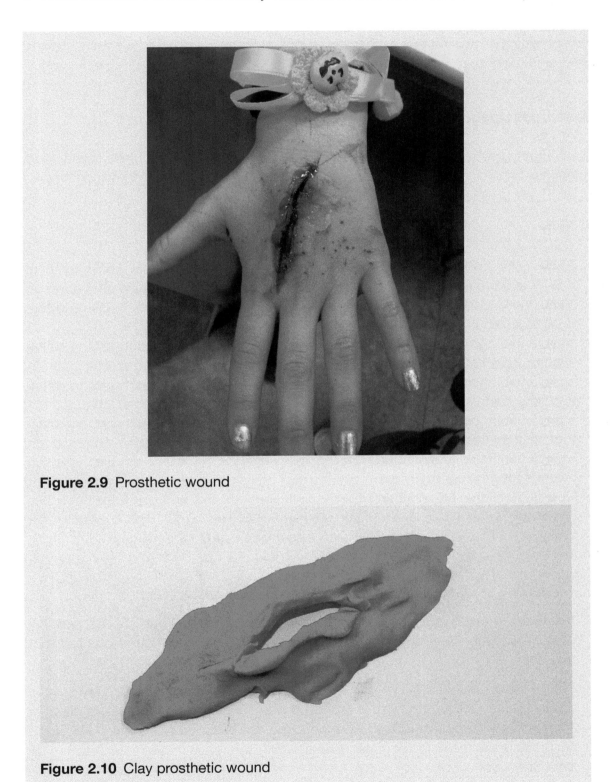

Figure 2.9 Prosthetic wound

Figure 2.10 Clay prosthetic wound

Prep for next session (slimy substance)

Try to source some disposable gloves for the next session

Session four
Slimy substances

Children always love the idea of making gloopy, slimy substances – especially when you tell them one of the substances is fake snot. Children will have lots of messy, gooey fun today creating slimy substances that would look at home in any special effects department or joke shop.

Resources needed

Slime/snot ingredients: PVA glue, water, bicarbonate of soda, contact lens saline, food colourings, including green; Oobleck ingredients: cornflour, water (cold); mixing bowls

Activity

1 Show children the image of green slime in Figure 2.11 and ask them what they think it is – the more creative the answers, the better. Explain that it is fake snot or green slime, the kind sold in joke shops or used in the movies. Ask children to give suggestions as to what might be in it

2 Reveal the ingredients (PVA glue, water, bicarbonate of soda, contact lens saline solution and food colouring) and get children to experiment with mixing them in small amounts to try and come up with a recipe ratio – how many parts glue to water, and how many teaspoons of bicarbonate of soda and contact lens saline solution? If any of them come up with a good recipe, get them to share it. Otherwise explain that children need to mix ½ cup of glue to ½ cup of water, then add ¼–½ teaspoon of bicarbonate of soda and one tablespoon of contact lens saline solution. Children select a food colour of choice

3 Now give children cornflour and coloured water to mix, exploring the substance they create. Note that it is called Oobleck (see Figures 2.12 and 2.13). How does this differ from the slime, and what special effects could it be used for? Sinking sand might be a good suggestion

   4–7 years – children follow the instructions and share observations

   7–9 years – children try to work out the slime proportions, but use the recipe if needed. They make observations about the mixtures, suggesting reasons for what they see

   9–11 years – children select their own ingredients. If unsuccessful after several attempts, they follow the recipe. They can also investigate the impact of different amounts of bicarbonate of soda on the slime. Children make observations about how the substances mix together using scientific language and offering reasons for what they see

Key questions

● How would you describe the Oobleck?
● What do you think has happened to the substances to make the slime?

Helpful hints

- Note: slime and Oobleck are non-Newtonian fluids, acting like solids and liquids
- Note: Oobleck responds to pressure that is applied to it and changes accordingly
- Note: contact lens saline solution contains an activator that changes the molecules of the glue causing them to tangle together

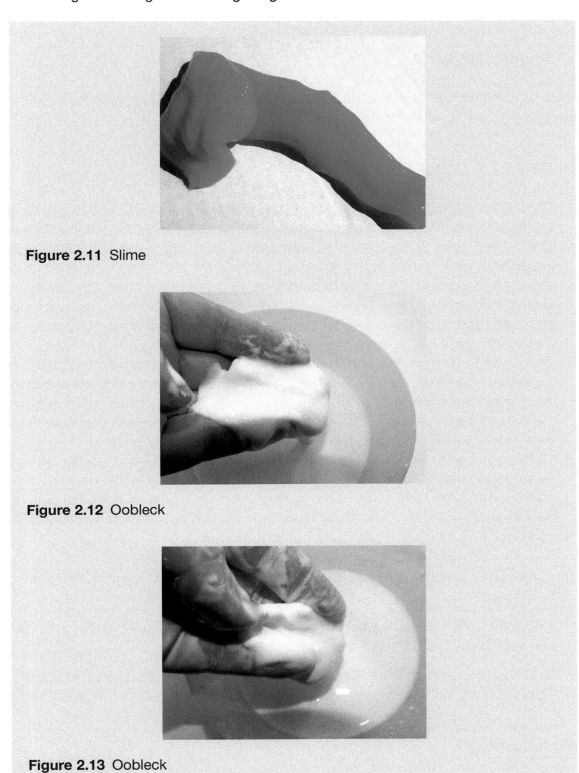

Figure 2.11 Slime

Figure 2.12 Oobleck

Figure 2.13 Oobleck

Prep for next session (light fantastic)

Challenge children to find some images of stained glass to share for the next session

Session five
Light fantastic

Today, children are going to explore one of nature's wonders: rainbows. They will then investigate coloured light mixing and see if they can create a stained glass window that changes the colour of the light beams shining through them.

Resources needed

Prisms; small mirrors; water; bowls; paper; torches; coloured tissue paper; coloured acetate gels or film; black card; glue sticks

Activity

1 Show children prisms and the effect of putting a mirror in water. Note that a rainbow is split light. See Figure 2.14 for the effect. Let them investigate the prisms and mirrors in water to try and identify the seven colours – red, orange, yellow, green, blue, indigo and violet
2 Explain that children are going to have a go at creating coloured light for themselves, but without using prisms or by splitting the light. Instead, they will use coloured filters to do the job, in the form of stained glass windows (see Figures 2.16 and 2.17)
3 Give children torches and coloured tissue paper or acetate gels and get them to experiment creating coloured light by covering the torch beams with these materials. Explain that coloured gels are used for lighting effects in theatres. Can they mix the colours if they cross the light beams? Children come up with light colour mixing rules – they are not the same as paint mixing rules (see Figure 2.15)
4 Children then use this colour knowledge, and any stained glass images they brought in, to design and make a stained glass picture using coloured gels on black card with cut-outs. They mix some of the gels to create new colours. Stick the pictures on a window – what happens to the light coming through? This is coloured light, not split light

4–7 years – children make simple observations and make suggestions for what they see

7–9 years – children make observations, suggesting reasons for what they see. They use scientific terms such as *translucent*, *light beam*, *filter*

9–11 years – children make detailed observations with related scientific reasons. They use scientific terms such as *translucent*, *light beam*, *spectrum*, *filter*, *split light*

Key questions

● Why has the light turned that colour?
● What happens if you mix two different colours?

Helpful hints

- Note: primary light colours are red, green and blue. Secondary colours are magenta, cyan and yellow
- Note: coloured gels block certain colours of the spectrum from passing through

Figure 2.14 Splitting light into rainbow colours

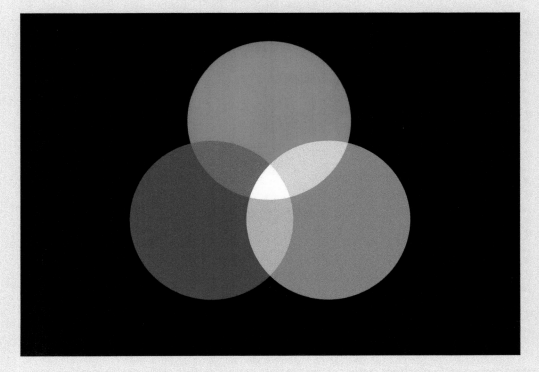

Figure 2.15 Mixing coloured light

Figure 2.16 Stained glass window

Figure 2.17 Stained glass window

Prep for next session (disco magic)

Ask children to bring in any old CDs they have at home that can be cut up

Session six
Disco magic

Exploring a hall of mirrors is always an entertaining, if somewhat disturbing, experience. Today, children are going to explore the nature of reflection with mirrors and see how they can be used to create an all-singing, all-dancing disco ball.

Resources needed

Mirrors; pens; paper; polystyrene balls; modelling clay; wooden skewers; glitter; CDs cut into small pieces; drawing pins; shiny paper or card cut into small pieces; PVA glue; torches

Activity

1 Give children a mirror and get them to write something on a piece of paper and see how it looks in each mirror. See Figure 2.18 for reference. Let them experiment with the mirrors, reflecting words and pictures. Ask them to describe what they see

2 Now challenge groups of children to send a beam of torch light from one end of a table to the other, reflecting it using multiple mirrors, to hit a target. Place paper on the table and see if children can draw the route of the beam. Can they move the beam to chase a target? Explain that theatres use mirrors to reflect and direct beams of light

3 Now ask children how they think a disco or glitter ball works. Show them Figures 2.19 and 2.20. Challenge them to try out different materials to make a disco ball using polystyrene balls or balls of modelling clay with a wooden kebab skewer stabbed into them as a base. Get children to decorate four balls with different materials to test out: glitter, chopped up CDs, brass drawing pins, and chopped shiny paper

4 Children test out their disco balls in a darkened room with torches as they twirl the ball on a wooden skewer

4–7 years – children describe, and perhaps use, the term *reflection*. They make simple observations about the different disco ball effects

7–9 years – children describe what they see in terms of reflection and light rays. They make observations about the different disco ball effects and offer suggestions for these

9–11 years – children describe what they see in terms of reflection, light rays, and angle of incidence. They describe the different disco ball effects using scientific language

Key questions

● How could you direct the light beam to hit a target?
● Why does a disco ball create such an impressive effect?

Helpful hints

● Soak the CDs in hot water before cutting as it makes them easier to cut
● Note: the Law of Reflection states that the angle of incidence is always equal to the angle of reflection

Figure 2.18 Mirror writing reflection

Figure 2.19 Disco ball

Figure 2.20 Glitter ball

Prep for next time

Have a look through and decide which topic you will do next time – the introduction page of each chapter will tell you what you need to prep

3 Environmental issues

Over the course of this block, children will consider a range of environmental issues of relevance to both their local community and the wider world. Experiments reinforce concepts in a child-friendly way and aim to leave children excited about the positive impact they as individuals can have on the world around them.

This block includes the following sessions (key resources underneath):

1 Reduce, reuse, recycle: plastic bottles

1-litre plastic bottles (one each); acrylic paint; wool; string; old magazines; fabric scraps; card scraps; PVA glue; paintbrushes; scissors; soil; nasturtium seeds

2 Reduce, reuse, recycle: rags

Old 'rag' clothes and socks; fabric and wool scraps; scissors; buttons; decorative scraps; fabric glue; thick card; marbles; hole punch

3 Oil slicks

Metal trays; water (coloured using food colouring); vegetable oil; tablespoons; sponges; flour; cotton wool balls; washing-up liquid; feathers; pipettes

4 Clean water

Water; soil; coffee filters; cheesecloth; sand; gravel; half-bottle funnels from Session one; plastic jugs; food colouring

5 Deforestation

Lego™; water; jugs; empty plastic bottles with one side cut out; soil; bark; cress in a bottle from 'prep for next session' from Session four; string; scissors

6 Clean energy

Box lids; black paper; plastic food bags; water; cellophane; Lego; lolly sticks; modelling clay; card; egg boxes; marker pens; wooden skewers; cotton reels; hairdryer; thermometer

In preparation for this block, it would be helpful to ask children to gather used plastic bottles and old ('rag') clothes. You will also need to use Lego in Sessions five and six, so it is worth sourcing this well in advance.

Session one
Reduce, reuse, recycle: plastic bottles

The unnecessary use of plastic is a topical issue in modern society. In this session, children consider the concept of reduce, reuse, recycle and create a re-purposed bottle planter, decorated with reused scraps, as they consider ways they can reduce their plastic footprint.

Resources needed

1-litre plastic bottles (one each); acrylic paint; wool; string; old magazines; fabric scraps; card scraps; PVA glue; paintbrushes; scissors; soil; nasturtium seeds

Activity

1   Show children a bag of collected plastic packaging and ask how long they think plastic takes to decompose. Explain that different plastics take different amounts of time: a plastic bag takes 20 years, while a plastic bottle takes 450 years. Highlight that plastic waste often ends up in waterways, blown from landfill sites, and then travels into our oceans, where it is having a devastating effect on marine ecosystems

2   Talk to children about the concept of reduce, reuse, recycle and ask what each of these terms mean. Bring out a plastic bottle and ask what they could do for each of these actions. They might suggest reusing water bottles for drink, recycling bottles where they can and reducing by buying a reusable bottle rather than one-use bottles

3   Explain that today children are going to reuse a water bottle by transforming it into a planter. Show children an empty bottle that has been cut in half. Explain that they will decorate the bottom half as their planter (see Figure 3.1) and will use the top half as a funnel in Session four. Make sure that the bottom half of the bottle has holes punctured into it to allow water to drain out

4   Show children the fabric scraps, noting that these are also being reused. Look at Figure 3.2 for an example, then give children free rein to decorate their planters as they wish. Once complete they fill the planters with soil and plant seeds

4–7 years – children design a simple planter. They relay the reduce, reuse, recycle concept, and identify one or two ways that they could cut down on their own plastic usage

7–9 years – children design a more intricate planter. They relay the reduce, reuse, recycle concept, and suggest ways they could cut down on their own plastic usage

9–11 years – children create an original and complex design for their planter. They understand the concept and implications of reduce, reuse, recycle for their own lives

Key questions

● What else could you use plastic bottles for?
● How could you cut down on your use of plastics at home?

Helpful hints

- Cover the cut edge of the bottles with masking tape to prevent cuts
- Note: by 2050, ocean plastic will weigh more than the weight of the fish living there

Figure 3.1 Decorating a bottle base planter

Figure 3.2 Bottle base planter

Prep for next session (reduce, reuse, recycle: rags)

Ask children to bring in any old 'rag' clothes they have that are ready for the charity shop

Session two
Reduce, reuse, recycle: rags

Reusing and repurposing old clothing can be hugely satisfying and surprisingly effective. Children will explore the idea of reusing fabric today as they embark on their own creative ventures.

Resources needed

Old 'rag' clothes and socks; fabric and wool scraps; scissors; buttons; decorative scraps; fabric glue; thick card; marbles; hole punch

Activity

1 Ask the children what happens when their clothes no longer fit. They could give them to someone else, take them to charity shops, pop them in a textiles recycling bag or reuse the fabric. Explain that children are going to have a go at repurposing some old rags today. Outline the following three options for children to choose from:
2 Sock puppet: see Figure 3.3. Children use old buttons, wool, card and other decorative scraps to create a sock puppet
3 Fabric bookmark: see Figure 3.4. Children take a strip of thick card and cut it into a bookmark shape. They cut fabric to a larger size than the bookmark and glue it onto the card, covering it with the raw edges tucked and glued in. Children may wish to punch a hole at the bottom and feed through a rag ribbon or wool to finish it off
4 Marble knot necklace: see Figure 3.5. Children cut a strip of fabric 50 cm × 10 cm. They leave 5 cm at one end and then tie a knot. They then place a marble or bead into the fabric, wrap it up and tie another knot tight in against the marble to hold it in place. They continue until their necklace is long enough
5 Challenge children to come up with other ways they could repurpose old clothes

    4–7 years – children make a sock puppet or a bookmark

    7–9 years – children make a sock puppet and a bookmark

    9–11 years – children make at least two of the items and come up with their own idea for a third project to complete

Key questions

- How else could you repurpose clothes?
- What does this fabric lend itself to in terms of a project?

Helpful hints

- If possible, use pinking shears to cut the fabric, as this will prevent it from fraying
- Note: over £140 million worth of clothing ends up in landfill sites every year

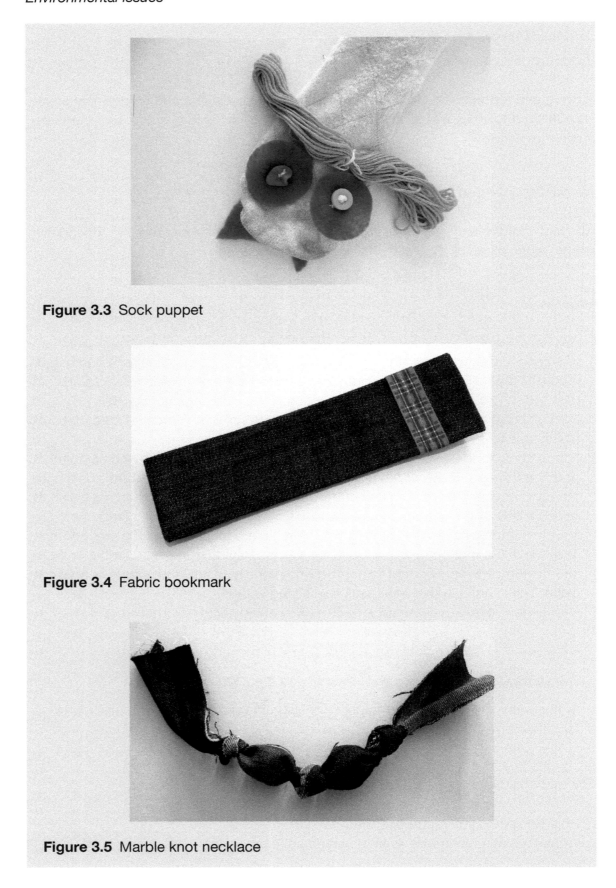

Figure 3.3 Sock puppet

Figure 3.4 Fabric bookmark

Figure 3.5 Marble knot necklace

Prep for next session (oil slicks)

Ask children to collect feathers for the next session

Session three
Oil slicks

Understanding the serious nature of oil spills in the ocean can be very tricky, as fortunately we don't often experience this first-hand. Today children will experiment with their own mini-oil spills to discover the effects of this environmental disaster and will try to find methods to clear it up.

Resources needed

Metal trays; water (coloured using food colouring); vegetable oil; tablespoons; sponges; flour; cotton wool balls; washing-up liquid; feathers; pipettes

Activity

1 In groups, children half-fill a plastic bottle with water then add some vegetable oil. Children shake it and describe what has happened. Oil and water don't mix. Eventually, the oil will settle on top of the water because it is less dense than water
2 Ask children how fuel oil is transported across the world. Explain that if oil tankers have accidents, oil can spill into the ocean and form an oil slick (see Figure 3.6). Such oil spills from ships can devastate local wildlife. Explain that today children are going to investigate ways to clean up an oil spill
3 In pairs, children pour coloured water into a metal tray then add 4 tablespoons of vegetable oil. They then set up an investigation to try to 'mop up' this oil spill using feathers, sponge, furry fabric, flour, cotton wool and pipettes (see Figure 3.7). Children note the impact of each mop-up item on the oil, but also the impact of the oil on the items. Can children relate any of the items to wildlife? Feathers from birds and fur from animals. How could children get the oil off of the feather? Try liquid soap
4 Share findings and explain that on a large scale, dispersants, which are chemicals, are used to break oil down oil so that water bacteria can decompose it

4–7 years – children make and record observations for each mop-up item

7–9 years – children make and record observations for each mop-up item. They offer reasons why each item behaves the way it does

9–11 years – children make and record observations for each mop-up item. They offer explanations using scientific language such as: *density*, *dispersal* and *molecules*

Key questions

● If there is an oil spill in the ocean, who should pay for the cleanup?
● What would be the impact of using chemicals to clear up oil spills?

Helpful hints

- Note: water molecules are more attracted to themselves than oil molecules
- Note: animals caught in oil spills struggle to regulate their temperature. It also poisons them, alongside plant life

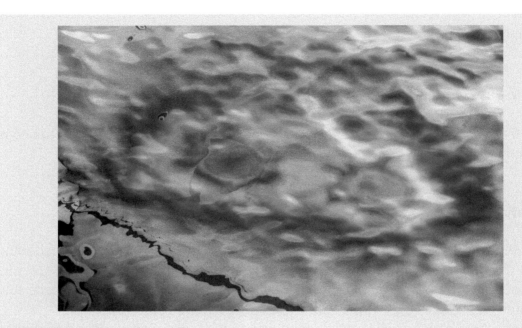

Figure 3.6 Oil slick

Figure 3.7 Oil experiment

Prep for next session (clean water)

You will need sand and gravel for the next session, which you may have to source in advance

Session four
Clean water

More than 700 million people around the world do not have access to clean water – a terrifying and mind-blowing number. With this in mind, today children will look at the complexities of the water purification process, and complete an investigation to try and find the best way to filter water.

Resources needed

Water; soil; coffee filters; cheesecloth; sand; gravel; half-bottle funnels from Session one; plastic jugs; food colouring

Activity

1   Do children think that all water sources (oceans, rivers, ponds) contain clean water? Which water sources may be unclean, and why? Highlight that over 700 million people worldwide don't have access to clean drinking water and often have to travel long distances to collect water. This is where purification systems can help. Explain that children are going to investigate one such system today
2   Challenge children to filter water which has been mixed with soil. They experiment with potential filters and record findings. Children test: coffee filter paper, cheesecloth, sand and gravel. They place each, one at a time, into the bottle funnels, then slowly pour in some of the water, letting the liquid drip through into a jug
3   Children note the colour of the liquid in comparison to the original. Which filter worked best? What happens if they use all four methods layered like a filter bed? (see Figure 3.10)
4   When finished, ask if the water is safe to drink. Show children coloured water and pour it through a filter. Note that because the food colouring is dissolved in the water, it can't be filtered out. Some impurities and bacteria in water won't filter, either, so the children's filtered water is not safe to drink. Note that where clean drinking water is scarce, dirty water can be purified using purification kits as well as filtering

4–7 years – children make and record observations for each filter

7–9 years – children make and record observations for each filter. They offer reasons for the success or failure of each one

9–11 years – children make and record observations for each filter. They offer explanations using scientific language such as: *dissolved*, *particles*, *mixture* and *suspension*

Key questions

● If you put food colouring in the water, could you filter this out?
● How would not having clean water affect your life?

Helpful hints

- Do not let the children drink any of the samples of water, even after filtering
- Aquarium sand and gravel work really well for this experiment

Figure 3.8 Collecting water

Figure 3.9 Collecting water

Figure 3.10 Layered filter

Prep for next session (deforestation)

Plant some cress in soil in a plastic bottle with one side cut out (see Figure 3.11 on page 52)

Session five
Deforestation

While major deforestation may not be happening on our doorstep, the global implications are huge. Not only does it increase levels of CO_2 in the atmosphere; it also causes soil erosion. Children will explore the effects of soil erosion today as they send a monsoon through some raw soil and deforest a Lego jungle.

Resources needed

Lego; water; jugs; empty plastic bottles with one side cut out; soil; bark; cress in a bottle from the 'prep for next session' from Session four; string; scissors

Activity

1   Discuss with the children the meaning of deforestation and where in the world it occurs. Can children identify what issues may arise from this? Explain how trees and plants can help protect the landscape from soil erosion, purify water and absorb CO_2

2   Demonstrate the impact of deforestation on soil erosion. Cut out one side of two large water bottles and fill one with soil and the other with the cress you prepped last week (see Figure 3.11). Place the two bottles next to each other with their necks hanging over the edge of a low table or wall with jugs underneath (see Figure 3.12). Water the soil until it trickles into the jug. Repeat with the cress. Children observe the differences between the water coming out. The plants help keep the soil clumped, preventing erosion

3   Now challenge children to investigate the impact of deforestation on run-off volumes, something which also impacts surface soil erosion. Challenge children to create a Lego forest with as many trees as possible (see Figure 3.13). Each tree must have a gap between it and the next one. Children then raise their forest onto a slant, pour a set amount of water onto to the top of it, and time how long it takes for the water to trickle down and through. Children investigate what happens as they remove ('chop-down') their Lego trees, removing a set number each time until there are none left

4–7 years – children record findings and make simple observations

7–9 years – children record findings and make observations based on these. They suggest the possible impact of bare ground on soil erosion

9–11 years – children look for a correlation between run-off time and number of trees. They describe the impact of bare ground on soil erosion using scientific language

Key questions

● How do the plants help prevent soil erosion?
● Can you think of other impacts from deforestation?

Helpful hints

● Note: other impacts from deforestation include loss of Indigenous communities and increases in methane gas, if the deforested land is used for cattle

Figure 3.11 Cress in a bottle

Figure 3.12 Water erosion experiment

Figure 3.13 Deforestation model

Prep for next session (clean energy)

Children to research different way we produce energy, in particular electricity

Session six
Clean energy

This week, children are going to be thinking about renewable energy sources. They will be racing wind powered cars, creating water turbines and heating water through solar power.

Resources needed

Box lids; black paper; plastic food bags; water; cellophane; Lego; lolly sticks; modelling clay; card; egg boxes; marker pens; wooden skewers; cotton reels; hairdryer; thermometer

Activity

1   Ask children how they think electricity is produced (hopefully, they will have researched this) and record their ideas in two 'mystery' lists (one *renewable* and one *non-renewable*). Do they know what you have done? Explain the difference between the two forms of energy. Explain that children are going to test some renewable energy today. Outline the following three options for children to choose from:

2   Solar collector: see Figure 3.14. Children set up a solar collector using a box lid lined with black paper. They check the temperature of some cold water which they then put in a sealed plastic bag and place in the box. They cover with cellophane wrap and leave in the sun for 30 minutes. After 30 minutes, children re-check the temperature of the water

3   Wind-powered car: see Figure 3.15. Children make a Lego car. They secure modelling clay in the middle and attach a lolly stick with a large square of card attached. Children use hairdryers to replicate the wind as they race their cars

4   Water turbine: see Figure 3.16. Children cut out six egg box cup sections (colour one with a marker – this is the indicator cup) and stick them onto the ends of skewers, which in turn are attached to a central cotton reel hub using modelling clay. Children place a long skewer through the cotton reel and put modelling clay on the end. This skewer works both as an axle and a handle for children to hold. Run the turbine under a steady, but gentle, flow of water and time how many rotations it completes in a minute, using the coloured cup for reference. Challenge children to get the highest number of rotations possible without the water shooting out everywhere

4–7 years – children make a wind car and solar collector. They describe what they see

7–9 years – children make a wind car or a water turbine. They also make a solar collector. They describe what they see and offer some suggestions for it

9–11 years – children make a wind car, a water turbine and a solar collector. They explain the processes using scientific language and offer improvement ideas

Key questions

● Will the size of the sail or blades change the amount of energy harnessed?

Helpful hints

● Complete the solar collectors first, so that they have time to work

Figure 3.14 Solar collector

Figure 3.15 Wind powered car

Figure 3.16 Water turbine

Prep for next time

Have a look through and decide which topic you will do next time – the introduction page of each chapter will tell you what you need to prep

4 Amazing bodies

Over the course of this block, children will explore and investigate their amazing bodies. They will make blood smoothies, investigate the science of finger printing, look at how the brain works and examine some remarkable measurements and biometrics.

This block includes the following sessions (key resources underneath):

1 **Blood smoothies**
   Smoothie ingredients: raspberries, small white marshmallows, sprinkles, pineapple juice, apples, blueberries, oranges; scales; bowls; forks; cups
2 **Fingerprints**
   Jars (washed with soap); a jar with your fingerprints on it; icing sugar; soft paintbrushes; ink; A5 paper or card; magnifying glasses
3 **Neurons**
   Rulers; paper; pencils; blindfold
4 **Optical illusions**
   Optical illusions; A6 pieces of paper; lolly sticks; glue sticks; paper discs; felt tip pens
5 **Body lengths and capacities**
   Water; two 5-litre water containers; 60 ml pot; tape measures; trundle wheels; string/ wool; chalk
6 **Investigating footprints**
   Roll of paper or sheets of sugar paper taped together with masking tape; water; sponge cloths

In preparation for each session in this block, make sure that you have read through the 'helpful hints,' which outline some of the science behind the activities.

Session one
Blood smoothies

Children begin this block in true gory style, by making a blood smoothie using ingredients that represent the contents of real blood. The red stuff pumping though our bodies is a fascinating substance, comprised of many different elements, and while drinking real blood is not recommended, these blood smoothies are a rather delicious, educational alternative.

Resources needed

Smoothie ingredients: raspberries, small white marshmallows, sprinkles, pineapple juice, apples, blueberries, oranges; scales; bowls; forks; cups

Activity

1 Ask children what their bodies are made from. Hopefully children will mention blood, but if not, prompt them to suggest it by asking what is pumping around their bodies. Can any (older) children tell you the main things found in blood? Explain that blood contains some important ingredients: red blood cells (carry oxygen), white blood cells (fight infection), plasma (transports nutrients) and platelets (clot blood)

2 Show children the blood smoothie ingredients and explain that there are 'main' ingredients that represent the key components of blood (red and white blood cells: berries and marshmallows, plasma: pineapple juice, and platelets: sprinkles)

3 Children make their blood smoothie. They use 100 g of berries and 130 ml of juice, with a pinch of the other ingredients. Older children add in antigen ingredients for their blood type (if known)

4 Children drink their smoothies and in groups come up with a savoury recipe for blood soup. They might suggest: stock (plasma), tomatoes (red blood cells), haricot beans (white blood cells), croutons (platelets). Older children suggest antigen ingredients

4–7 years – children are aware that blood contains various components and that it transports oxygen and helps fight/prevent infection

7–9 years – children are aware that blood contains various components, and can name some. They know explain that it transports oxygen and helps fight/prevent infection

9–11 years – children know and name the various components of blood. They explain how it transports oxygen and helps fight infection. Children use additional antigen ingredients (to help fight infection and determine our blood group): apples (A), blueberries (B) and oranges (O) antigen ingredients

Key questions

● What do the different ingredients represent?
● What are some of the main functions of blood?

Helpful hints

● Note: deoxygenated blood is not blue, despite its appearance through our skin. Oxygenated blood is bright red and deoxygenated blood is dark red

Figure 4.1 Raspberries

Figure 4.2 White mini marshmallows

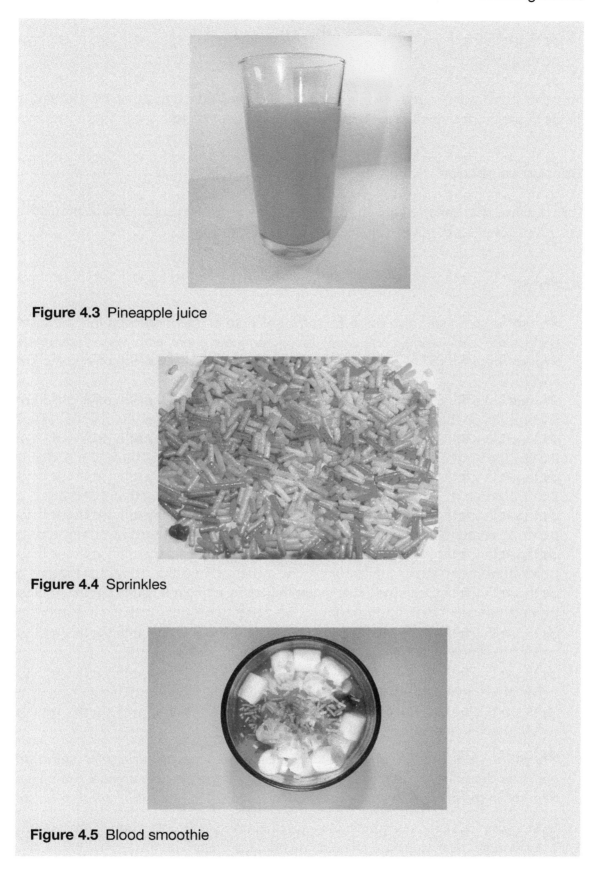

Figure 4.3 Pineapple juice

Figure 4.4 Sprinkles

Figure 4.5 Blood smoothie

Prep for next session (fingerprints)

Collect empty glass jars for next week – ask children to bring in any from home, as well

Session two
Fingerprints

Today, children will assume the role of classic storybook detectives, dusting for finger-prints in search of a solution to 'The Case of the Mixed-Up Jars.'

Resources needed

Jars (washed with soap); a jar with your fingerprints on it; icing sugar; soft paintbrushes; ink; A5 paper or card; magnifying glasses

Activity

1   As children come in, give them each a jar to hold in their fingertips (not clasped). Collect the jars, being careful not to contaminate them with your fingerprints. Explain that children need to work out whose jar is whose. Do they have any idea how?

2   Share a collective lightbulb moment as you realise that the jars have the children's fingerprints on them. Discuss how you might be able to recover them from the jars. Show children the items you have and identify the icing sugar as a dust to cling to the grease on the jars made by their fingers. Look at Figures 4.6–4.8 and identify patterns

3   Show children how to dust an example jar (with your fingerprints on) and ask how they could create a record of everyone's prints to compare these with. Use ink and paper to create a fingerprint card for each child, labelling each with the relevant child's name. These will be available for all children to reference

4   Children work in pairs, trying to identify the owners of two jars. They dust the jars for prints and then compare with the fingerprint cards, using magnifying glasses. When they are confident that they have found the correct print card they put it with the jar. Make sure children compare their jar prints with all the fingerprint cards, as they may find some similar prints that they will have to study closely

4–7 years – children describe fingerprints using simple language. They roughly draw the shapes they can see on the jar print pattern onto paper to help identify the cor-rect patterns in the print

7–9 years – children describe fingerprints using descriptive language. If they strug-gle, they draw the shapes of the jar prints onto paper to help identify the correct patterns in the print

9–11 years – children describe the fingerprints using the terms whorl, loop and arch. They identify the matching prints directly from the dusted prints

Key questions

● How would you describe the shapes in the fingerprints?
● Do they match exactly?

Helpful hints

- Note: fingerprints are formed from skin layers that are twisted together
- Note: identical twins do not have matching fingerprints

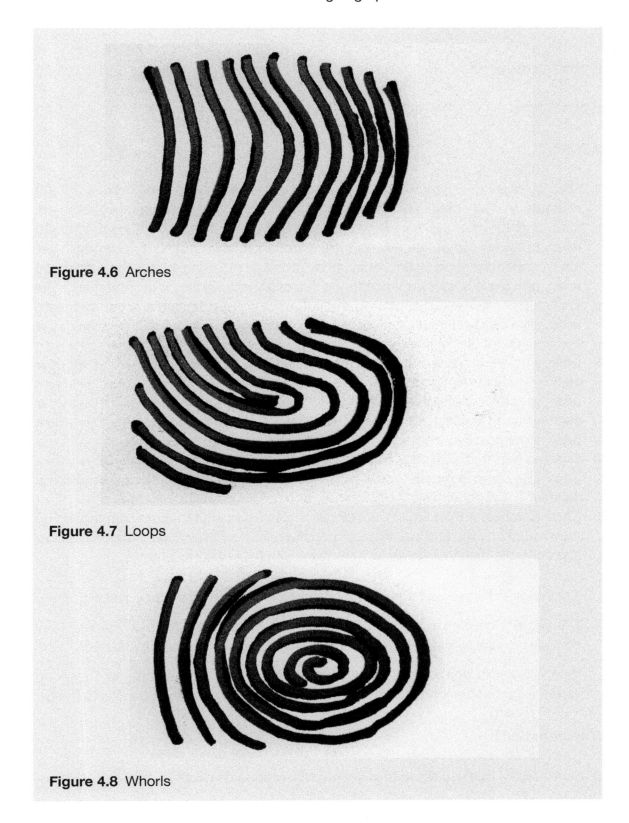

Figure 4.6 Arches

Figure 4.7 Loops

Figure 4.8 Whorls

Prep for next session (neurons)

Arrange to have a large space available (a hall or outdoor area) for the next session

Session three
Neurons

Children will be getting their neurons firing this week, testing their reactions, as they investigate how different stimuli affect their speeds of response.

Resources needed

Rulers; paper; pencils; blindfold

Activity

1   Start by playing a game of 'neuron snakes' in a large space. One child is 'it' and chases the others until they tag someone. That child holds their hand and runs with them until they tag another. They continue until they have a long enough chain to reach between two points (labelled 'burning candle' and 'brain'). Explain that they have created a neuron chain, meaning the message ('burning candle') can reach the brain, provoking a 'reflex' response – in this case, moving the away from the candle

2   Explain that reflexes – like moving away from pain – are involuntary, but that reactions – like catching a ball – are conscious. Children will explore their own reactions by carrying out an investigation

3   Children work in pairs: one is the dropper and the other the catcher. The dropper stands and holds a ruler at the 30 cm point while the catcher sits and holds their hand near the zero cm point (see Figure 4.9). The dropper drops the ruler while the catcher catches it (see Figure 4.10). Children read and note down the point on the ruler where the catcher grabbed the ruler. They repeat five times, then swap roles

4   Children can then calculate their responses using Table 4.1. Note that this was a visual cue creating the reaction. Children repeat the investigation with a blindfolded catcher. The dropper calls 'now' as they drop it. This is an auditory cue

5   Children repeat a third time. The catcher is still blindfolded, but they are tapped on the shoulder by the dropper as they drop the ruler – a physical cue. Children record and calculate their responses and compare with their other results

4–7 years – children complete challenges and record responses and times

7–9 years – children complete challenges and record responses and times. They compare results with others and suggest what happens to cause the reaction

9–11 years – children complete challenges and record responses and times. They analyse findings and explain what happens to cause the reaction using scientific language

Key questions

● Do you think that you could train yourself to respond quicker?

Helpful hints

● Note: neurons have an all-or-nothing response
● Note: we create faster responses as our neuron chains are fired over and over

Figure 4.9 Ruler investigation 1

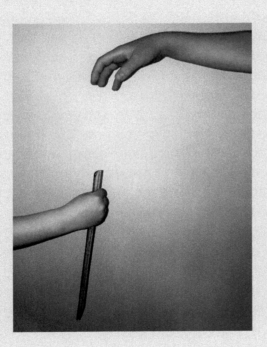

Figure 4.10 Ruler investigation 2

Table 4.1 Ruler experiment response times

Distance	Time
5 cm	0.10 seconds
10 cm	0.14 seconds
15 cm	0.17 seconds
20 cm	0.20 seconds
25 cm	0.23 seconds
30 cm	0.25 seconds

Prep for next session (optical illusions)

Challenge children to find some examples of optical illusions at home to bring in

Session four
Optical illusions

This week is going to get confusing, as children investigate a range of optical illusions, looking at how they trick the brain. They will then attempt to create some of their own.

Resources needed

Optical illusions; A6 pieces of paper; lolly sticks; glue sticks; paper discs; felt tip pens

Activity

1 Explain that because our brains use short cuts to interpret things around us, we are sometimes tricked into seeing something that we can't explain. These are called optical illusions

2 Share some examples that you and the children have brought in (see 'prep for next session' from Session three). See also Figures 4.11 and 4.12. What can children see, and how do they know that it is an illusion? Explain that children are going to have a go at creating their own illusion today that will trick the brain into thinking one thing when the reality is very different

3 Model how to draw a cat on one piece of A6 paper or card, and a basket on another. The basket should be positioned on the page so that if the cat picture were on the same piece of paper, it would be sitting in the basket. Stick the pictures back to back, with a lolly stick or straw stuck between them. Then roll the stick or straw back and forth between your hands so that the images whizz back and forth. What happens to the cat? It looks like it is sitting in the basket

4 Children create their own version of this illusion. They choose two things that might ordinarily be together in a picture, but draw them separately. They can experiment with as many as they like

5 Then challenge children to do the same but this time they use discs or paper and colour them different colours, using felt tip pens. What happens when they are spun?

4–7 years – children describe what they see

7–9 years – children describe what they see. They make suggestions as to what might be happening

9–11 years – children describe what they see using expressions such as: *optical illusion*, *messages to the brain* and *visual confusion*

Key questions

● Why do you think your brain thinks the cat is in the basket?
● Why do the colours mix?

Helpful hints

● Note: the brain interprets what the eye sees when you look at an optical illusion. The brain gets very confused by what it is seeing

Figure 4.11 Optical illusion

Figure 4.12 Optical illusion

Prep for next session (body lengths and capacities)

Make sure that you have plenty of trundle wheels and tape measures available for next time

Session five
Body lengths and capacities

The lengths, capacities and areas of some parts of our bodies are mind blowing. Today, children are going to explore some of these measurements and look at experiencing and recreating what some of them look like in reality.

Resources needed

Water; two 5-litre water containers; 60 ml pot; tape measures; trundle wheels; string/wool; small food bags; chalk

Activity

1 Help children to point to where their intestines are. Clarify that this is where food is digested and absorbed, and waste is separated out. How long do children think it is? An adult small intestine is 6–7 metres long, while the large (wider) intestine, is about 1.5 metres long. That's a lot of intestine! Explain that children are going to work in three groups to explore this and other body measurements
2 Set one group to work measuring and cutting a piece of one colour of wool to the length of the small intestine. Do the same with a different colour of wool for the large intestine. Encourage them to lay out the pieces to appreciate how long this, then ask them to find a way to squash it into a small food bag – just like it is in the body
3 Give the second group the two 5-litre containers, one full of water, the other empty, and a 60 ml pot. They have one minute to transfer the water from one container to the other, using the small pot. Five litres is the volume of blood pumped around the body every minute
4 The third group draws the total surface area of one adult lung in chalk on the ground outside. This is about 30 square metres, which is a rectangle 10 metres by 3 metres
5 Once finished, the groups swap activities. All groups should complete all activities, then carry out some age-specific calculations (see ahead)

4–7 years – children measure as per the instructions. They add the length of the small intestine to the large intestine. They also work out the area for both lungs and how much blood is pumped around the body in 15 minutes

7–9 years – children find different ways to show the area of one and then two lungs. They calculate how many litres of blood the heart pumps around the body in an hour

9–11 years – children work out different ways to show the area of one and then two lungs. They calculate how many litres of blood the heart pumps around the body in a day

Key questions

● Why is it useful to have such a long small intestine?
● Why does the area of the lungs need to be so great?

Helpful hints

● When creating the lung area, get children to mark the corners of the rectangle first

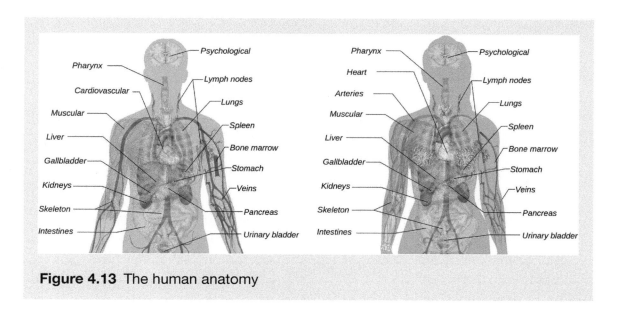

Figure 4.13 The human anatomy

Prep for next session (investigating footprints)

Ask children to draw around their feet and cut them out to bring in for next session

Session six
Investigating footprints

Today, children will be getting their shoes and socks off as they explore their amazing feet, looking at what happens to them when we walk, run, jump and even dance.

Resources needed

Roll of paper or sheets of sugar paper taped together with masking tape; water; sponge cloths

Activity

1   Get children to take off their shoes and socks, and describe their feet in detail to a partner. Ask them if they know why they are designed the way they are and whether we all have identical feet. Share children's cut-out footprints that they have hopefully brought with them

2   Get children to stand on a sponge cloth in water, then to step onto a piece of paper. How do the footprints they create differ from one another? Note that some people have what are called high arches and others have medium or low arches. People also have different widths of feet

3   Explain that children are going to investigate their feet today by carrying out various activities and seeing what they notice about their footprints. To record this, they will use large rolls or sheets of paper (firmly stuck down) and water

4   In groups, children investigate walking, running, dancing, jumping and hopping, to see which parts of their foot touch the ground (the foot-strike) and the distances between their footprints and the position of the feet

5   Each group can carry out their investigation as they wish, but need to report back on their findings and try to explain what they have discovered

    4–7 years – children describe their findings and make some simple suggestions for them

    7–9 years – children describe their findings in detail and make suggestions for them

    9–11 years – children describe their findings in detail and make scientific suggestions for them that reflect biometrics

Key questions

● Why does that part of your foot hit the ground most or first when running?
● How does your foot-strike differ from other people?
● Why are the feet together when you jump but apart when you run?

Helpful hints

● Note: when you run, the foot-strike differs from person to person. Some strike with the front of the foot, others with the side and others with the heel

Figure 4.14 Run

Figure 4.15 Dance

Figure 4.16 Jump

Figure 4.17 Hop

Prep for next time

Have a look through and decide which topic you will do next time – the introduction page of each chapter will tell you what you need to prep

5 Maths in nature

In this block, children will explore the mathematics of the natural world. They will look at symmetry, shapes and patterns, and will use their measuring skills to further examine the natural world. Children will also consider how nature uses addition and multiplication to thrive and grow.

This block includes the following sessions (key resources underneath):

1 **Shapes in nature**
   Leaves of different shapes; paper; masking tape; colouring pencils; felt tip pens; shells
2 **Angles in nature**
   Sticks and twigs (straight, bent and with branches); masking tape; marker pens; poster paints
3 **Symmetry in nature**
   Leaves; marker pens; glue sticks; pencils; air-drying clay; sets of nature items (leaves, petals, seed casings, etc.); paper plates
4 **Patterns and fractals**
   Examples of fractals (or just use Figure 5.6); drawing pencils and pens; paper
5 **Measuring nature**
   A3 paper; poster paints; paintbrushes; cubes for measuring; rulers; tape measures; string; squared paper
6 **Addition and multiplication in nature**
   150 g packet of sunflower seeds; compound leaves with a range of 'leaflet' numbers

In preparation for this block, ensure that you have access to a natural outdoor space. Also gather together a range of nature items and measuring equipment.

Session one
Shapes in nature

Shapes in nature are both functional and beautiful. In this block, children will create some patterned artwork based on leaf and shell shapes, while learning some intriguing leaf shape names.

Resources needed

Leaves of different shapes; paper, masking tape; colouring pencils; felt tip pens; shells

Activity

1 Ask children what shape leaves are (without looking at any). Then explore the leaves that you have collected and note how some are oval, some are heart-shaped, some are round, some are oblong and so on
2 Look at the leaf shapes in Figures 5.1–5.3 and challenge children to find a range of similarly shaped leaves outside. You may be limited by the natural area available, but try to encourage children to use shape terminology and bring back contrasting shapes
3 Once children have collected leaves, challenge them to repeatedly draw around each to form a pattern. Older children can see if they can tessellate the shapes (see Figure 5.4). Children then add colour repetition to their patterns using colouring pencils or felt tip pens
4 Children can explore other patterns and shapes in nature, such as in shells. They repeat this process, looking to tessellate the shapes and add patterns where possible

   4–7 years – children describe shapes including key properties. They try to tessellate shapes

   7–9 years – children attempt to use correct mathematical terms for shapes and note key mathematical properties. They tessellate shapes

   9–11 years – children use correct mathematical terms for shapes and note key mathematical properties. They tessellate multiple shapes

Key questions

● Can you think of anything else with a similar shape?
● How could you turn the shapes to make them slot together?

Helpful hints

● Children can make card templates of their leaf shapes if it makes drawing around them easier
● Use masking tape to stick the corners of the paper to the table to keep it still

Figure 5.1 Cordate leaf shape

Figure 5.2 Ovate leaf shape

Figure 5.3 Lanceolate leaf shape

Figure 5.4 Leaf tessellation

Prep for next session (angles in nature)

Ask children to bring in sticks for next time – including straight, bent and branched

Session two
Angles in nature

Having explored shapes in nature last week, in this session children are going to think about the range of angles generated by the natural world. They will explore the irregularity of sticks and twigs, thinking about the angles they create. Children will create an angle art sculpture using their sticks.

Resources needed

Sticks and twigs (straight, bent and branched); masking tape; marker pens; poster paints

Activity

1 Let children explore the sticks and twigs that you and they have collected. Focusing on one stick each, get them to describe the shapes and bends they see, using language such as *turns*, *bends*, *angles*
2 Challenge them to see if they can join a number of sticks together to create a complete shape. Explain, though, that they can only have a corner or turn in their shape if the branching or direction of the stick or twig allows it (i.e. they can't create a right angle by putting the ends of two sticks together; see Figure 5.5 for an example)
3 Children experiment with a range of stick creations, and when they are happy with the final layout, they join their sticks together using masking tape
4 Now challenge children to highlight on the sticks, in marker pen, where all the angles are. Older children can use a protractor to measure the angles and add them up
5 Children then paint their angled shape sculpture to create a piece of branching art
6 If time permits, children can make a second sculpture

> **4–7 years** – children describe the angles in terms of turns and directions
>
> **7–9 years** – children describe the angles in terms of partial turns and directions
>
> **9–11 years** – children measure the angles and use mathematical language to describe them

Key questions

● How will the angle change the overall shape of your sculptural layout?
● What impact do big or small angles have on the overall shape of your structure?

Helpful hints

● To get more branched sticks, you could prune a garden bush in advance to select specific branches

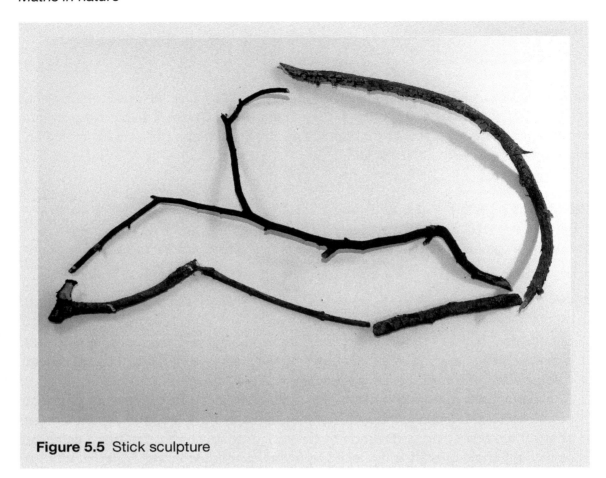

Figure 5.5 Stick sculpture

Prep for next session (symmetry in nature)

Ask children to collect sets of similar leaves and other nature items such as petals and seed casings

Session three
Symmetry in nature

This week, children are looking for symmetry in nature. While they will be familiar with butterfly and flower symmetry, this week they will be exploring the intricacies of leaf symmetry and trying out artistic techniques that enable them to re-create missing, symmetrical halves.

Resources needed

Leaves; marker pens; glue sticks; pencils; sets of nature items (leaves, petals, seed casings, etc.); paper plates

Activity

1 Set up children in groups with a range of leaf shapes and ask them to draw any lines of symmetry they can spot with a marker pen
2 Children then each choose a leaf and cut down one of the lines of symmetry
3 They stick half of their leaf in the middle of a page and fold the page in half to create the line of symmetry. Then children attempt to draw the other symmetrical half. What could children do that would help to make the overall shape accurate? Suggest that older children use measured lines to work out how far out from the line of symmetry the drawn half needs to come (see Figure 5.6)
4 Children complete their drawing, then cut out the whole shape and fold down the centre line to see how close they have come to creating a symmetrical shape
5 Additionally you can give children a paper plate and challenge them to create a nature symmetry plate using various nature items, as in Figure 5.7

   4–7 years – children use simple leaf shapes and make symmetry plates using two types of very different items

   7–9 years – children use more complex leaf shapes and make symmetry plates using three types of very different items

   9–11 years – children use very complex leaf shapes and make symmetry plates using a wide range of items, some of which are similar

Key questions

● How could you draw the other half accurately?
● How will you place each identical item to ensure that it is symmetrical?

Helpful hints

● Children should place items on their plate first and glue once they are sure of their positioning

Figure 5.6 Drawing leaf symmetry

Figure 5.7 Symmetry plate

Prep for next session (patterns and fractals)

Ask children to try and take notice of overall tree shapes and branch shapes they encounter over the next week

Session four
Patterns and fractals

Some patterns in nature are very obvious – a bee's stripes or a leopard's spots, for example. But do you (or the children) know that trees grow in patterns, too? In this session, children will be introduced to the concept of fractals and the ways in which trees replicate according to mathematical rules.

Resources needed

Examples of fractals (or just use Figure 5.8); drawing pencils and pens; paper

Activity

1   Show children examples of fractals, either your own or Figure 5.8. What can they see? Hopefully they will suggest it is a repeating, growing pattern. Explain that this is a fractal. Fractals are patterns that grow by following a mathematical rule
2   Now challenge children to pick a shape and then to make up a simple mathematical rule for its growth and repetition. For example, they might start with a circle that then grows to the right and doubles in size (see Figure 5.9 for an example)
3   Show children Figures 5.10–5.12 and explain that within these trees, there are lots of repeating shapes that follow a mathematical rule. Note that the overall shape of the tree is the same as the shape of each of its individual branches. Trees are fractals, too. Explain that children are going to explore tree fractals today and create their own fractal art, based on a tree in your outdoor space or working from a picture
4   Children try and spot the basic shape that is repeated and draw it. They then add in branches that are the same shape, and then branches on the branches, again following the same pattern (see Figure 5.13). They could use a different colour for each level of the pattern, i.e. brown for the main tree shape; green for the large, first-level branches; and red for the smaller, second-level branches
5   Children can have a go at drawing two or three different trees if time permits

4–7 years – children use very simple tree shapes

7–9 years – children complete two tree fractals with more complex shapes, then make up a fantasy tree fractal

9–11 years – children complete two tree fractals with complex shapes, then make up a fantasy tree fractal

Key questions

● How does the size and direction of the shape change within the fractal tree?
● Can you design your own complex fractal tree?

Helpful hints

● Note: fractals repeat branching shapes. Mathematically, they are very complex

Figure 5.8 Fractal

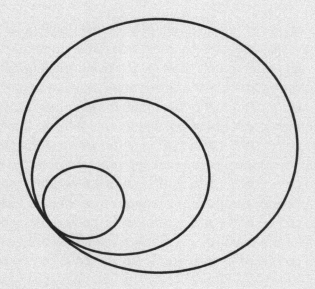

Figure 5.9 Simple repeating growth pattern

Figure 5.10 Tree fractal

Figure 5.11 Tree fractal

Figure 5.12 Tree fractal

Figure 5.13 Tree fractal drawing

Prep for next session (measuring nature)

Ask children to collect leaves for next time

Session five
Measuring nature

Today, children are going to get their rulers out and put some of their local leaves to the measuring test. Which leaves are the longest, widest, have the longest circumference, and even the oldest? Children will print the results for analysis.

Resources needed

Leaves of differing size and shape; A3 paper; poster paints; paintbrushes; cubes for measuring; rulers; tape measures; string; squared paper

Activity

1   Challenge children to select no more than five or six of the leaves you have collected or that they have hopefully brought in, and to put them in length order. Using paint, get them to print the leaves in that order along the top of a sheet of A3 paper and label it 'length.' Use a different colour for each leaf. Then children repeat for width measurements, again printing the leaves in order. They should print this strip under the 'length' strip (see Figure 5.14)

2   Now challenge children to put the leaves in order of circumference length. Can they think of an easy way to measure this? Offer them string to see if that prompts them to place the string around the circumference and then measure the length of the string. Again, children print a strip of leaves in order

3   Next up is the age of the tree that the leaves came from. How could children do this? Explain that while you cannot cut the trees down to count the rings, there is a trick that works for most trees. If they measure the circumference of the widest part of the trunk in inches, this number is an approximation of the age of the tree in years. Children print the results, again using the leaves from each tree to represent the order. Children can then compare the orders and see where each leaf has come in each category. Is there a clear winner?

    4–7 years – children measure in non-standard units (cubes), if necessary, and have help measuring circumferences. They note any leaves that are consistently 'winning'

    7–9 years – children measure accurately using standard units. They note the orders and ascribe points to first, second and third place in order to work out an overall winner

    9–11 years – children estimate then measure accurately. They create a fifth printed strip for the area of leaves that they work out using squared paper. Children note the orders and ascribe points to first, second and third place in order to work out an overall winner

Key questions

● Are the orders the same? Why not?
● How long do you think it is in centimetres?

Helpful hints

● You could also explore range, mean and median measures with older children

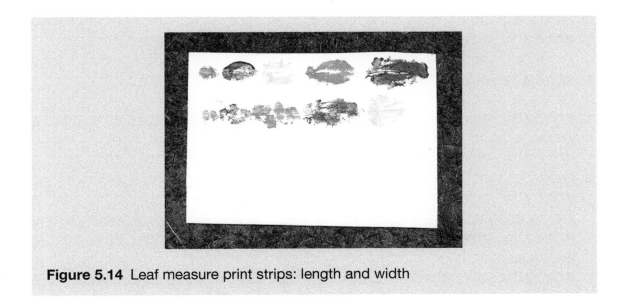

Figure 5.14 Leaf measure print strips: length and width

Prep for next session (addition and multiplication in nature)

Find compound leaves (see Figures 5.15–5.17) for next session. Ask children to look for some as well

Session six
Addition and multiplication in nature

Today, children will be exploring the ways that trees and plants add and multiply. They will help to solve some huge calculations, and will try to calculate the number of leaves on a tree.

Resources needed

150 g packet of sunflower seeds; compound leaves with varying small leaf (leaflet) numbers

Activity

1 Ask children how many seeds they estimate that one sunflower head contains. Record ideas, then note it is between 1,000 and 2,000 seeds (the amount in your seed packet)
2 Now ask: if only 100 of these seeds grew into new sunflower plants, how many sunflower seeds would there be altogether, assuming each new sunflower plant had one head? Hopefully children will suggest 100 × 1,000 (or 2,000, depending on the size of the sunflower head). That is 100,000 seeds – that's a lot of seeds that initially started off from one plant!
3 Children are now going to think about the compound leaf in Figure 5.17. How many small leaves (leaflets) does each leaf have? If each whole leaf has five small leaflets within it and a young tree starts with ten leaves, how many small leaves are there altogether? Note that 10 × 5 = 50. What if that tree doubled its leaves every year for ten years?
4 Challenge older children to investigate the answer and to work out how many years it would take for there to be over 50,000 leaflets. Younger children complete the investigation by looking at a tree with one leaf of five leaflets which doubles each year. How many leaves after seven years, and how long to get to over 1,000 leaflets? Children then investigate for trees with leaves of three, seven and nine leaflets
5 Once finished, head outside to do some leaf counts. Older children work out: leaves on a twig × twigs on a branch × number of branches. Which tree has the most? Younger children total the branches of a given tree species to see which has the most

   4–7 years – children use addition

   7–9 years – children use multiplication

   9–11 years – children use multiplication and more complex numbers

Key questions

● How could we work out the number of leaves on a real tree?

Helpful hints

● If children struggle with the maths, get them to draw the leaves as they multiply

Figure 5.15 Horse chestnut compound leaf

Figure 5.16 Acacia compound leaf

Figure 5.17 Virginia creeper compound leaf

Prep for next time

Have a look through and decide which topic you will do next time – the introduction page of each chapter will tell you what you need to prep

6 Sensational structures

Over the course of this block, children will find themselves faced with an array of structural challenges, employing a remarkable range of components to overcome them.

This block includes the following sessions (key resources underneath):

1 **Tall towers**
   An array of building materials: boxes, tubes, lolly sticks, pots, newspapers, straws; PVA glue and glue sticks; sticky tape; scissors; A2 or A1 sugar paper
2 **Food architecture**
   Edible structure examples; jelly sweets; toothpicks; books of different sizes and weights
3 **Building bridges**
   Images of bridges; newspapers; sticky tape; pennies; books of different sizes and weights
4 **Marble run mania**
   Video of a huge marble run (widely available online); cardboard tubes; various types of sticky tape; marbles; stop watch; sandpaper; aluminium foil; cellophane
5 **Rain chains**
   Water source; jugs or watering cans; chain links or strong wire; buckets or bowls; decorative items: malleable wire; pine cones; plastic cable ties; metal or plastic 'scrap' (old cutlery, keys, etc.)
6 **Indoor dens**
   Sheets or tarpaulin; pegs; strong string or washing line cord; chairs

In preparation for each session in this block, gather together the building materials needed, ensuring you have excess for when a structural disaster strikes.

Session one
Tall towers

When we think of tall towers, many famous buildings spring to mind: the Eiffel Tower, Big Ben and the Empire State Building, to name only three. Today, children will build their own memorable towers from a range of experimental materials.

Resources needed

An array of building materials: boxes, tubes, lolly sticks, pots, newspapers, straws; PVA glue and glue sticks; sticky tape; scissors; A2 or A1 sugar paper

Activity

1 Show children the photos of the towers in Figures 6.1 and 6.2, and ask how the shapes and structures differ. Note that the Eiffel Tower has lots of open triangular and criss-cross metallic shapes that taper towards the point at the top, while Big Ben is a solid cuboid structure made from stone
2 Get children into groups of three and challenge them to create a tall tower. Explain that they need to try and create as tall and stable a tower as they can with the 'experimental' materials available. They can choose a structure similar to either the Eiffel Tower or Big Ben, or they can come up with their own structural ideas
3 Children choose their materials and plan out their ideas before building their tower on a sheet of sugar paper
4 Once all towers have been completed, get children to visit one another's towers and decide which they think is the tallest and most stable
5 Find your winning tower by measuring the tower heights then testing their stability by wobbling the sugar paper they have been built on

   4–7 years – children either use the Eiffel Tower or the Big Ben structure

   7–9 years – children either use the Eiffel Tower or the Big Ben structure, but adapt it and add their own ideas

   9–11 years – children use their own ideas to design the tower. Also challenge this group to make their towers as interesting as possible to look at

Key questions

● Why have you chosen these materials?
● How could you make it more stable?

Helpful hints

● Make the towers on the ground to ensure that children don't create unnecessary risk by standing on chairs
● Note: some of the most stable structures in the world have unexpected shapes. The key to stability is the spreading of the loads from the overall structure

Figure 6.1 The Eiffel Tower

Figure 6.2 Big Ben

Prep for next session (food architecture)

Purchase toothpicks and jelly sweets and create edible structure examples for next session

Session two
Food architecture

After their maverick approach to building design in Session one, it is now time for children to learn a little about the science and maths behind architecture and structural engineering, specifically looking at load bearing and force transferral. To do this, today they will be building edible structures.

Resources needed

Edible structure examples; jelly sweets; toothpicks; books of different sizes and weights

Activity

1 Share your own edible structure examples and show children Figures 6.3–6.5. Ask them what shapes have been created – and how. Explain that the cube, the pyramid and the triangular prism have all been made using sweets and toothpicks
2 Challenge children in pairs to have a go at creating some three-dimensional shapes using sweets and toothpicks. Once they have made a shape, see if they can add to it to make a bigger structure. Ask children why the structure holds together. Explain that pushing and pulling forces keep it stable and solid
3 Now ask children to make a flat square and a flat triangle. Can they move the sides and change the shape? They can with the square – it becomes a diamond – but not with the triangle. Note that triangles are very strong structures. Think back to Session one and the Eiffel Tower
4 Using their jelly sweets and toothpicks, challenge children to construct a strong building made up of triangles. Get them to think about the sort of building it will be, and what they want the overall shape to be. Children then test the load-bearing capabilities of their constructions by adding weight to them – books work well for this purpose

   4–7 years – children build simple structures and make observations

   7–9 years – children build simple structures and make observations. They make suggestions as to what might be happening with the loads and forces

   9–11 years – children build more complex structures. They describe what they see using scientific terms such as *push*, *pull*, *tension*, *equal forces* and *load*

Key questions

- How do you think it stays strong?
- Why do you think triangles are a good shape to use?

Helpful hints

- Note: where something is pulled, it is called tension; where something is pushed and squashed, it is called compression

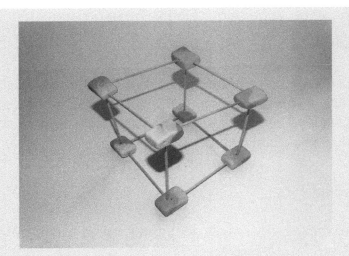

Figure 6.3 Sweet and toothpick cube

Figure 6.4 Sweet and toothpick prism

Figure 6.5 Sweet and toothpick pyramid

Prep for next session (building bridges)

Ask children to find pictures of bridges, and bring some old newspapers to the next session

Session three
Building bridges

Having learnt the basics of a strong structure during the last session, children are going to apply their knowledge this week as they try to build a bridge big enough and strong enough to span the gap from one desk to another. . . at height!

Resources needed

Images of bridges; newspapers; sticky tape; books of different sizes and weights

Activity

1   Share your images of bridges and look at those children may have brought in. Can they spot any that look like the sweet structures they made in Session two? Figure 6.7 shows a truss bridge, which is a good example of such a structure
2   What other structural forms can they see in the images? Why do they think these structures are strong and don't collapse? Remind children of the role of forces in structures and that the pushes and pulls need to be equal. Bridges also need to be able to take load and spread it effectively so that they don't collapse
3   Challenge children in groups of three to create their own bridge using rolled, taped newspaper that will span the distance between two desks without collapsing. Show children how to roll the newspaper to make it a stronger structure to build with. Explain that they can go for any design they like, but that it should be based on one of the bridges they have seen today
4   Once children have built their bridge, they need to test it with some loads (books work well) to see how strong it is

4–7 years – children build simple structures and make observations

7–9 years – children build simple structures and make observations. They make suggestions as to what might be happening with the loads and forces

9–11 years – children build more complex structures. They describe what they see using scientific terms such as *push*, *pull*, *tension*, *equal forces* and *load*

Key questions

● How have you made it stay strong?
● How do you think it spreads the weight of the load?

Helpful hints

● Note: bridges support loads by spreading the weight out through either compression alone, or compression and tension

Figure 6.6 Truss bridge

Figure 6.7 Forth Bridge

Prep for next session (marble run mania)

Ask children to bring in any cardboard tubes they have at home

Session four
Marble run mania

Everyone loves a marble run – and quite frankly, the bigger, the better. This week, children are going to have a go at creating the biggest, longest marble run possible using cardboard tubes. Children will need to think carefully about their structures, though, to make sure they can harness the force of gravity.

Resources needed

Video of a huge marble run (widely available online); cardboard tubes; sticky, masking and duct tapes; marbles; stop watch; sandpaper; aluminium foil; cellophane

Activity

1　Show children a video of a huge marble run. Ask why the marble travels so far on the run. Note that gravity pulls things down towards the earth, which is what is happening to the marble
2　Divide children into two teams. Explain that each will build its own marble run. The rules are simple: the structures must stay standing, and the marble must flow easily along the run. The team whose marble takes the longest to complete the run wins. Show children Figures 6.8 and 6.9 for ideas
3　Children work together to build their marble runs. Support and advise children, and help them to time the run of their marbles. Suggest that children might try to make their marble runs interesting to look at

4–7 years – children build a simple structure. They describe what they observe and offer an explanation for the marble moving

7–9 years – children build a more complex structure. They describe what they observe and explain why the marble moves using the term *gravity*. Challenge them to include a 'speed bump' in their run, whereby momentum will keep the marble going

9–11 years – children build a complex structure which changes direction. They describe what they observe and explain the science behind why the marble moves, using the term *gravity*. Children include 'speed bumps' in their run and experiment with different internal surfaces to see how they affect the speed of the marble (sandpaper, aluminium foil, cellophane)

Key questions

● Why does the marble keep moving?
● What if sandpaper lined your run? Would the marble go faster or slower?
● Does the angle of the chute have an effect on the speed of the marble?

Helpful hints

● You can alternatively use foam pipe insulation for the chutes
● The chutes don't need to be attached to each other. They can be attached to a wall or table, as long as the marble falls from one to the other

Figure 6.8 Marble run

Figure 6.9 Marble run

Prep for next session (rain chains)

Ask children to bring in any old cutlery, keys, plastic or metal 'scrap,' or decorative items
to be used in the next session – these items will not be returnable

Session five
Rain chains

Rain chains are a decorative but functional addition to an outdoor space. They enable water to flow out of guttering into a water butt, drain or porous ground (essentially, they replace a downpipe). Children are going to have a go at creating a rain chain today, and will test them out to see if they can channel water to a specific spot.

Resources needed

Water source; jugs or watering cans; chain links or strong wire; buckets or bowls; decorative items: malleable wire, pine cones, plastic cable ties, metal or plastic 'scrap,' old cutlery or keys, etc.

Activity

1 Ask children to remind you how their marble runs worked during Session four. Explain that today they are going to be creating a structure that moves water from roof guttering to a point on the ground. Show them Figure 6.10 and ask what is happening to the rain water. Explain that this is a rain chain and its purpose is to channel water from one place (e.g. guttering) to another (perhaps a water butt)
2 How do children think it works? Explain that gravity pulls the water down and that it 'clings' to the structure as it offers a path for the water
3 Show children the available building materials and explain that they need to create a 'chain' using wire or cable ties, then add decorative items. Model how to bend the wire and twist the end to create a link (a bit like making paper chains). See Figure 6.11 for ideas, and explain that decorative items need to be added as they build the chain (not afterwards)
4 Children work in threes to create their rain chains, then test them by pouring water from a jug or watering can. Find somewhere functional to hang the chains

   4–7 years – children describe what they observe in simple terms

   7–9 years – children describe what they see and suggest that *gravity* causes the water to fall. They predict what might happen if they use more or less decorative items

   9–11 years – children describe what they see and explain what is happening. They use scientific language including *gravity* and *path of least resistance*. Children also predict what might happen if they use more or less decorative items. Challenge children to improve the design of their chain to make the water even more focused on the end point

Key questions

● Why do you think the water follows the rain chain?
● What would happen if you added more or less decorations to the rain chain?

Helpful hints

● Make sure that items are securely fixed, as water may force them apart

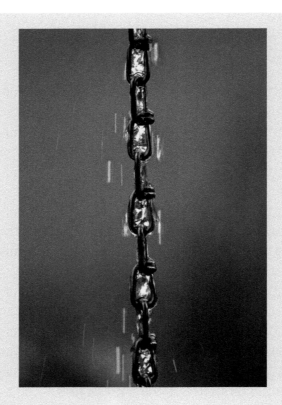

Figure 6.10 Chain with water

Figure 6.11 Rain chain

Prep for next session (indoor dens)

Bed sheets or tarpaulin are required for the next session – if children can't help, charity shops are often a good source

Session six
Indoor dens

No rainy day is complete without an indoor den building adventure. In this session, children are going to attempt to create the ultimate den, using sheets as their main building material.

Resources needed

Sheets or tarpaulin; pegs; strong string or washing line cord; chairs

Activity

1   Ask children if they have ever made an indoor den. What did they use, and how did they ensure that it was strong, stable and fully enclosed? Take ideas and make a list. Show them Figure 6.12, and note the materials used and the way that the tarpaulin has been secured
2   Explain that children will work in teams of four to build a den. The main criteria that they have to meet are that they can all fit in the den, that it has an opening and closing entrance, that it doesn't easily collapse and that at least one member of the team can stand up straight in it
3   Give children access to sheets, pegs, chairs and cord/string. Challenge them to think about ways to raise the roof of their structure and how to connect sheets securely to structural items. Remind children that they will need to ensure that forces are equal to ensure stability
4   Once children are happy with their dens, test them against the given criteria

    4–7 years – children have help securing cord/string. They use simple scientific and problem-solving language in their discussions

    7–9 years – children work independently. They use scientific and problem-solving language in their discussions

    9–11 years – children work independently. They use scientific and problem-solving language in their discussions, including the language of forces. Their dens are stable and meet all criteria

Key questions

● Why does the sheet keep falling down?
● How could you secure the sheet?
● How could you make it higher and more stable?

Helpful hints

● Two parallel cords give the structure better head height

Figure 6.12 Indoor den

Prep for next time

Have a look through and decide which topic you will do next time – the introduction page of each chapter will tell you what you need to prep

7 Outdoor skills

Over the course of this block, children will explore nature and learn some basic outdoor survival skills. The block can be completed at any time of the year, although autumn, spring and summer will offer a wider choice of materials to use.

This block includes the following sessions (key resources underneath):

1 Solar ovens
Cardboard pizza box; pencil; ruler; scissors; aluminium foil; sticky tape; black paper; cellophane; transparent plastic bag; newspapers; oven gloves; aluminium tray; crackers; cheese; chocolate; sticks

2 Den building
Long sticks; trees with low branches; outdoor string; tarpaulin or old sheets

3 Tying knots
Pieces of rope

4 Map reading
Site maps; paper strips; pens and pencils; compasses

5 Twig plates
Twigs and sticks; twine

6 Outdoor scavenger hunt
Plant/leaf identification sheets; paper; pens; pencils; cameras

In preparation for this block, ensure that you have an outdoor space available in which to work. Session one needs to be completed on a sunny day, so you may need to shuffle the order around at the last minute. Alternatively, children could make the ovens and take them home to try out themselves when the weather permits. If you don't have access to large sticks and branches for den building (Session two), children could use tubes and hung washing lines. You will also need to familiarise yourself with the knot-tying techniques for Session three.

Session one
Solar ovens

Cooking outdoors is one of life's great treats, and while fire building is a skill in its own right, today children are going to build an environmentally friendly solar oven and cook up a treat.

Resources needed

Cardboard pizza box; pencil; ruler; scissors; aluminium foil; sticky tape; black paper; cellophane; transparent plastic bag; newspapers; oven gloves; aluminium tray; crackers; cheese; chocolate; sticks

Activity

1   Ask children how people cook outdoors. Most likely they will suggest barbecues, fires and maybe even pizza ovens. But what about a solar oven? Can children guess what heat source this uses to cook with?
2   Explain that solar ovens trap the sun's energy, using dark paper to absorb heat and a transparent heat trap to prevent it from escaping. How might aluminium foil be used to improve the power of a solar oven? It can be used to reflect light into the heat trap
3   In groups, children set up a solar oven using a pizza box (see Figures 7.1–7.3). They cut three sides of a square from the top and fold it back as a lid. They line the base with black paper and cover the inside of the lid with aluminium foil. When ready to cook, children can put their food (chocolate or cheese on a cracker) inside and cover it with cellophane. On a warm day, chocolate or cheese will melt within 20 minutes
4   While their food is cooking, show children how to make a fire from sticks (see Figure 7.4). Do children know what fire needs to burn? Dry fuel and oxygen. Encourage children to make a small fire with clear air gaps and a ring of small rocks around it to contain the fire. Explain that this is a method of outdoor cooking that uses wood as its fuel. If time permits, you could light one of the fires to cook marshmallows, but ensure that you have water or a fire blanket on hand
5   Children check on their solar oven food after 20 minutes and eat their snack outside

4–7 years – children make the oven and describe what happens

7–9 years – children make the oven and describe how they think it works using terms like *reflect*, *absorb* and *heat energy*

9–11 years – children make the oven and describe in scientific language how it works using terms like: *reflect*, *absorb* and *heat energy*. They make improvement modifications

Key questions

● How does the aluminium foil help the oven?
● How else could you improve the oven's efficiency?

Helpful hints

- Children mustn't touch the hot oven with their bare hands during or after cooking
- Don't leave the ovens unattended, as they could pose a fire hazard

Figure 7.1 Solar oven part 1

Figure 7.2 Solar oven part 2

Figure 7.3 Solar oven part 3

Figure 7.4 Fire building

Prep for next session (den building)

Try to locate some large sticks for outdoor den building next week

Session two
Den building

Having worked out how to cook food outdoors, children are going to spend time today attending to another basic need: shelter. Using natural materials to create their dens, they will need to consider the best possible shapes and structures to ensure their structures survive against the elements.

Resources needed

Long sticks; trees with low branches; outdoor string; tarpaulin or old sheets

Activity

1 Beyond food and water, ask children what is important to have in the outdoors if you are sleeping overnight, or the weather is very hot, very cold, rainy or snowy. The answer is shelter. Ask if any children have done woodland den building before. If they have, get them to outline their experiences and share any advice they may have

2 Show Figure 7.5 and ask what the children are doing. Can they suggest any methods or materials that are being used to create the shelters? Note the use of the inverted V-shape, created by laying sticks against a tree trunk or large branch. Highlight that sticks are laid in an alternating pattern, first from one side, then the other

3 Explain that children are going to work in two teams today to build an outdoor den that they can all fit in. Suggest that they use Figure 7.5 for inspiration, but also come up with their own ideas as they look at the materials and space available to them. One of the keys to successful den building is being able to work with what you have, so it is important that children can improvise and adapt their structure as obstacles arise. Den building is all about problem-solving and team-work

4 Head outside and look at the materials available. Children gather together sticks and have access to string and either tarpaulin or sheets to drape over their den once complete. Children can examine one another's dens and note any areas for improvement

4–7 years – children focus on the basic inverted V-shape structure

7–9 years – children use the inverted V-shape structure and use string where needed to secure the den

9–11 years – children use the inverted V-shape structure and use string where needed to secure the den. Challenge children to create a den with two separate indoor areas, and to make improvements as they go

Key questions

- What will happen if it rains?
- How have you made the structure strong?

Helpful hints

- If you don't have an appropriate outdoor area or materials, use tubes and hung washing lines to mimic the sticks and branches

Figure 7.5 Den building

Prep for next session (tying knots)

Familiarise yourself with the knots for Session three (see Figures 7.6–7.9 on page 115–116)

Session three
Tying knots

From making shelters to setting up washing lines, the art of tying knots never goes a miss in the great outdoors. Today, children will learn to tie four different knots and have a team knot-tying competition.

Resources needed

Pieces of rope

Activity

1 Give children a length of rope and ask them to tie a knot – have a look at what they come up with. Any children who tie an interesting or complex knot should share their method with the others. Why do children think it is useful to be able to tie knots? Shelters, water collection systems, washing lines or even rescue missions need good knots for successful outcomes

2 Explain that children are going to spend today learning how to tie four knots (photocopy Figures 7.6–7.9 for reference). Work through each knot in turn, until children have mastered them all, explaining their uses as you go

3 The reef knot is useful for tying up a bundle of wood, to make a washing line longer, or for securing bandages. The bowline knot could be used to tie a food bag to the end of a rope so that it can be slung over a tree branch. The figure-eight knot is good for towing cars out of mud, while the hitch knot is great for tying a line to a tree or a load to a car

4 Children get into teams to practice their knots in practical contexts (see suggestions in instruction 3). Then hold a knot-tying competition for each knot – teams get a point for every child who has formed the knot correctly

4–7 years – children focus on accuracy over speed. They have a go at using them in action

7–9 years – children focus on accuracy and speed. They use them in action with accuracy

9–11 years – children focus on accuracy and speed. They use them for multiple purposes accurately

Key questions

● Why is the knot good for this purpose?
● How else could you use this knot?

Helpful hints

● If children struggle to follow the guidance, talk through the knot as you make it: 'up and over, through and down.' Make it into a chant

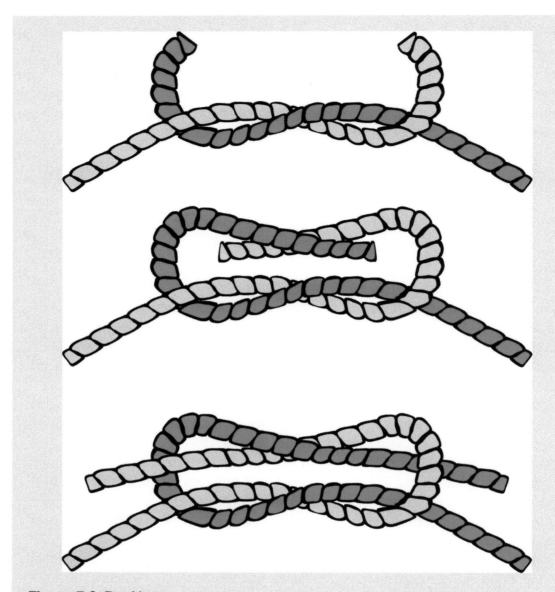

Figure 7.6 Reef knot

Figure 7.7 Bowline knot

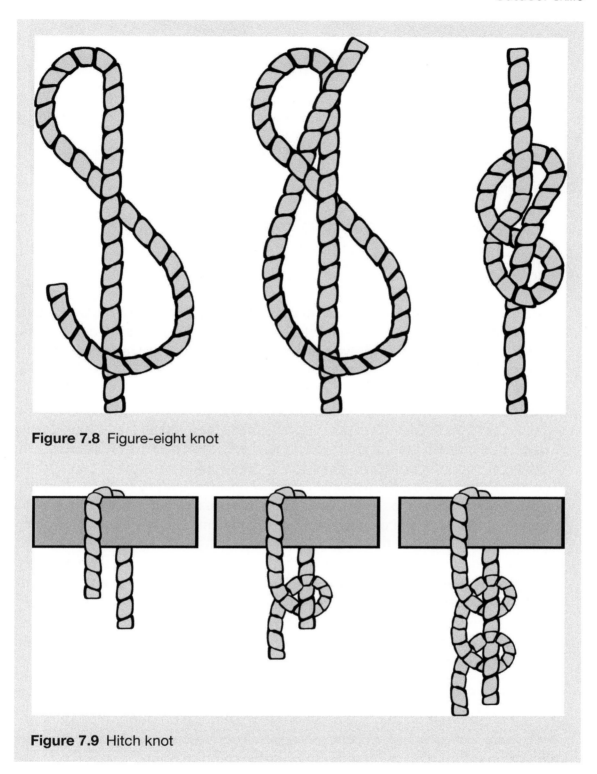

Figure 7.8 Figure-eight knot

Figure 7.9 Hitch knot

Prep for next session (map reading)

Ask children to bring in any local area maps they have (especially OS maps)

Session four
Map reading

Having eaten, set up camp and tied up washing lines in the previous sessions, it's finally time for some exploring. This week, children will use maps and compasses to design their own treasure hunts.

Resources needed

Site maps; paper strips; pens and pencils; compasses

Activity

1 Use a compass to identify and clearly mark north. Play a game of 'North, South, East, West' where children turn to face the relevant direction as you call them out. For older children use south-west, north-west, south-east and south-west, as well
2 Ask children why it is important to know how to read a map and use a compass when you are on an outdoor adventure. Emphasise that getting lost can be very dangerous. Look at the maps that children have hopefully brought in and find your location. Also, note the symbols used and the key. Show them the site map and note your location
3 Explain that children are going to work in teams to design their own treasure hunt, devising a route with up to five 'treasures' or pieces of information to be collected. They mark the path on a site map and create symbols for any key features. They then create directional clues or instructions using compass points. For example, a clue might read: 'travel north from the junior playground until you reach the bench. What is the name of the tree to the west of the bench?'
4 Children then swap clues and try out each other's treasure hunts. On a blank copy of the site map, they draw the route they follow based on the clues given, to see how closely it matches the original

4–7 years – children use north, south, east and west. They describe distance in approximate steps

7–9 years – children use eight compass points. They describe distance in approximate metres. 'Treasures' include the common names of trees and flowers

9–11 years – children use 16 compass points. They describe distance in whole and partial metres (e.g. 10.6 m). 'Treasures' include the common names of trees and flowers

Key questions

- Were the directions accurate?
- Did you find any trees or plants difficult to identify?

Helpful hints

- Children can draw their path on the map as they follow the instructions

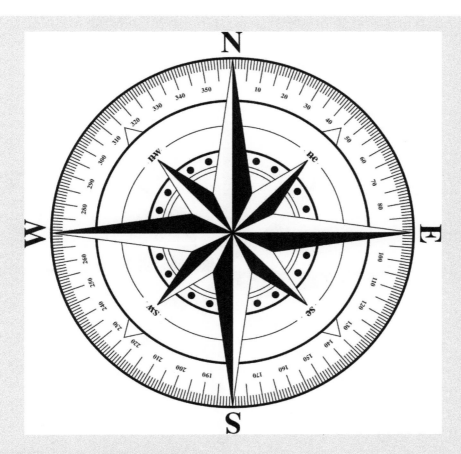

Figure 7.10 Four-point compass

Figure 7.11 Eight-point compass

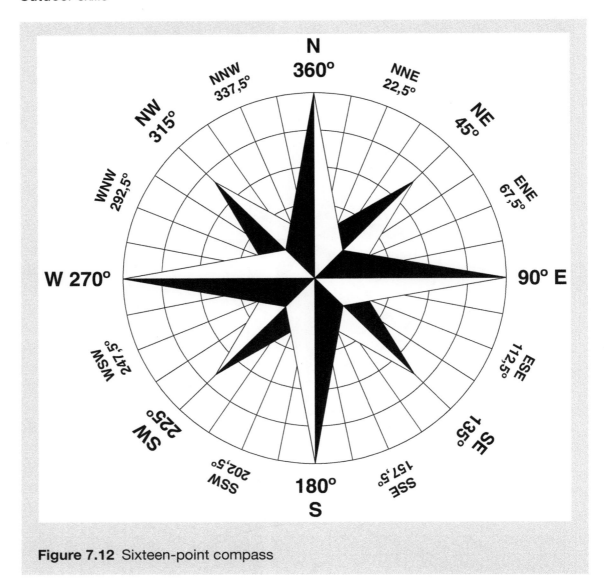

Figure 7.12 Sixteen-point compass

Prep for next session (twig plates)

Ask children to find twigs and sticks to bring to the next session

Session five
Twig plates

Children should be feeling very at home in the great outdoors by now, so today they are going to create some twig plates to put things like hot pans or bowls of food on, using the natural resources that they might find on an outdoor adventure.

Resources needed

Twigs and sticks; twine

Activity

1 Show children Figure 7.13 and ask what it is made from and how it has been put together. Explain that it is a twig plate for putting pans or plates on when you are camping or on an outdoor adventure. Note that it is bound together with twine
2 Lay out two sticks parallel to each other, with between eight and ten sticks lying perpendicular across them (see Figure 7.14)
3 Then show children how to use the twine to bind the sticks together, starting off with the figure-eight knot learnt in Session three (see Figures 7.8 and 7.15). Explain that children need to do this at both ends, but can work out their own method of winding the twine around the middle twigs in order to attach them
4 Children then create their own twig plate

    4–7 years – children use six crossed twigs spread out to allow easier access when binding the twigs

    7–9 years – children use eight to ten crossed twigs which are closer together

    9–11 years – children use as many crossed twigs as they can fit in – these should be as close together as they can be

Key questions

● What else could you make using this method?
● What could you use to bind the twigs together if you didn't have twine?

Helpful hints

● Encourage children to make different twig items if time permits

Figure 7.13 Twig plate

Figure 7.14 Laying out twigs

Figure 7.15 Binding the twigs

Prep for next session (scavenger hunt)

Ask children to research common native trees and plants in preparation for devising and taking part in a scavenger hunt during the next session

Session six
Outdoor scavenger hunt

To round off this block, children are going to design a scavenger hunt for your outdoor area. There are many ways to amuse yourself in the great outdoors, but scavenger hunts are always a good source of entertainment.

Resources needed

Plant/leaf identification sheets; paper; pens; pencils; cameras

Activity

1 Send children off on a quick mini-scavenger hunt. Challenge them to find two different types of leaves, a twig and a rock. When they come back, explain that they are going to design their own nature scavenger hunt, but that they will need to be more specific in their list of things to find
2 Show children the oak leaf in Figure 7.16 and ask them which tree it comes from. Once they have established it is from an oak tree, explain that their scavenger hunt needs to include this kind of level of detail – hopefully they will have done some research and know some local plants and trees
3 Send children off in groups to identify between five and ten items to include on their list (see Figure 7.17 for examples of items they might include) and help them to identify any unknown leaves or items. Use leaf identification sheets if available
4 Then challenge children to add in something that is a rogue item, that couldn't possibly be on the list as it doesn't grow or cannot be found in the local area – for example, a cactus spine is unlikely to be found in a school garden area
5 Once completed, children swap lists and get hunting. Which list contains the most challenging items?

    4–7 years – children identify common plants on their list and may refer to rocks and stones by shape

    7–9 years – children identify common plants on their list and may refer to rocks and stones by colour, texture or shape

    9–11 years – children identify common plants on their list and may refer to rocks using the terms *igneous*, *sedimentary* or *metamorphic*

Key questions

● Does the shape of the leaf help you to identify it?
● Which things did you find especially hard to find?

Helpful hints

● Children photograph items that would otherwise need picking

Figure 7.16 Oak leaf

Figure 7.17 Items in a scavenger hunt

Prep for next time

Have a look through and decide which topic you will do next time – the introduction page of each chapter will tell you what you need to prep

8 Electrical and magnetic wonders

Over the course of this block, children will explore some fun and quirky uses for electricity and magnetism – certainly not what they are likely to encounter in their conventional science lessons. They will discover and investigate ways in which these forces can be harnessed to create toys, games and magical effects.

This block includes the following sessions (key resources underneath):

1 Magnetic fireworks

Magnets; coloured pipe cleaners; scissors; empty transparent jars or bottles with lids; small metal items (paper clips, coins, etc.); mineral water

2 Magnetic slime

PVA glue; contact lens saline solution; food colouring; mixing bowls; paper plates; spoons; iron filings; magnets; plastic sandwich bags (to transport slime)

3 Static art

Pre-made tissue paper butterfly (see instruction 3); empty drinks can; balloons; tissue paper in variety of colours; glue sticks; scissors; cardboard

4 Bug-bots

Toothbrush heads (snap the tops off and cover any sharp edges with masking tape); small circular batteries; small motors; sticky pads; connecting wires

5 Buzzers and bulbs

'Operation' game; electricity kits, including bulbs and buzzers; copper wire; modelling clay or old plastic containers

6 Graphite circuits

Examples of graphite circuit images; graphite pencils (one sharpened at both ends); 9-volt batteries in cases; LEDs; sticky tape; plain paper

Magnets and electrical circuitry are integral to this block, so before embarking on it, it might be sensible to check these are readily available to you.

Session one
Magnetic fireworks

Children begin this block with a bang, as they use lowly pipe cleaners to create fireworks in a jar. Instead of using matches, though, it is a magnet that sparks this particular spectacular into life.

Resources needed

Magnets; coloured pipe cleaners; scissors; empty transparent jars or bottles with lids; small metal items (paper clips, coins, etc.); mineral water

Activity

1   Ask children what their favourite fireworks are and how they work. Highlight the bright colours and explosive movements and sounds, as well as establishing that they are fuelled by fire. Explain that children are going to create a similar effect today, but on a much smaller scale and without the use of fire
2   Show children a jar or bottle with a lid, mineral water, the magnets and the pipe cleaners. Explain that this is all they need to create their fireworks in a jar, but don't explain how it is made or how it will work. Challenge children to work out in pairs how they could use the equipment they have to create something that moves magnetically around inside the jar
3   Hopefully children will realise that the pipe cleaners are magnetic and that if the magnet is moved around the outside of the jar, the pipe cleaners will move with it. The water provides a medium for the pipe cleaners to move through
4   What other 'bits' could they add that would also work with the magnet? Children suggest and add in other items such as paper clips, coins and any other pieces of metal you have available. Children gather their firework items, and twist and twirl their pipe cleaners to make them look more interesting, before making their fireworks in a jar

   4–7 years – children describe the attraction of the metal in the pipe cleaners to the magnet. They suggest alternatives that might work in their jar (e.g. coins, paper clips)

   7–9 years – children describe the attraction of the metal in the pipe cleaners to the magnet using the term *force*. They also note that the magnet doesn't have to be touching the pipe cleaner to attract it. They suggest alternatives that might work in their jar

   9–11 years – children describe magnetic force using scientific terms such as *attract* and *repel*. They also note that the magnet doesn't have to be touching the pipe cleaner to attract it. Children can try different liquids (e.g. oil, fizzy water) to see which works best

Key questions

- Did the length of pipe cleaner affect the strength of magnetism?
- Are there any other investigations you could do with the pipe cleaners?

Helpful hints

- Note: magnets attract because they exchange photons

Figure 8.1 Magnetic fireworks in a jar

Prep for next week (magnetic slime)

One of the ingredients for next week is contact lens solution – you may need to buy this

Session two
Magnetic slime

Staying with magnetic forces, today children will create another fun effect by creating slime that can be controlled with a magnet. The magic ingredient is iron filings, which children will add to their slime to allow it to be coaxed into life.

Resources needed

PVA glue, water, bicarbonate of soda, contact lens saline solution, food colouring; mixing bowls; paper plates; spoons; iron filings; magnets; plastic sandwich bags (to transport slime)

Activity

1 Have any of the children made slime before? Discuss methods if they have. Explain that today they are going to make magnetic slime. What do they think this does, and can they suggest what you might put in it to make it magnetic?
2 Discuss a range of possible magnetic metal forms that could be added (paper clips, pipe cleaners, etc.), but note that these wouldn't result in a very smooth substance. Show children the iron filings and explain that these are magnetic, but are much smaller than many other magnetic items
3 Children are now ready to make their own magnetic slime, using the following method: mix ½ cup of glue to ½ cup of water, then add ¼ teaspoon of bicarbonate of soda and 1 tablespoon of contact lens saline solution. Children add food colouring and a heaped spoonful of iron filings. Use a spoon to combine the ingredients
4 Once the slime has been created, children can put it onto a paper plate and hover a magnet above it. What do they think will happen?

4–7 years – children describe the attraction of the iron filings in the slime to the magnet

7–9 years – children describe the attraction of the iron filings in the slime to the magnet using the terms *force* and *attract*. They also note that the magnet doesn't have to be touching the slime to attract it

9–11 years – children describe magnetic force using scientific terms such as *attract* and *repel*. They also note that the magnet doesn't have to be touching the slime to attract it. Children experiment with how different sized bodies of slime (small pieces and large expanses) respond to magnets, predicting what they think might happen

Key questions

● Which ingredient makes the slime magnetic?
● Do you think the slime will behave differently if it is in lots of small pieces?

Helpful hints

- Remind children that the slime mustn't be eaten and that they should wash their hands after playing with it

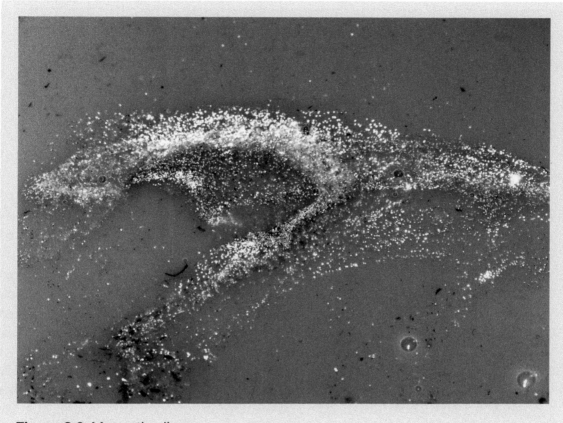

Figure 8.2 Magnetic slime

Prep for next week (static art)

Pre-make a tissue paper butterfly for the next session and test out making it move with a 'charged' static balloon – you will need this as a demo

Session three
Static art

Having focused on magnetic forces during the last two sessions, this week children will explore static electricity and the attraction it creates. Children will be able to amaze their friends with a magical piece of art that moves when a 'charged' balloon is hovered over it.

Resources needed

Pre-made tissue paper butterfly (see instruction 3); empty drinks can; balloons; tissue paper in variety of colours; glue sticks; scissors; cardboard

Activity

1 Have a drinks can sitting out on the table and ask children how they could move it without touching it. Make a list of ideas that might include: 'use a magnet', 'blow it with a hair drier' or 'bang the table until it falls over'
2 Lay the drinks can horizontally on a flat surface and rub a blown up a balloon back and forth on your hair to create static energy. Place the balloon near the can (without touching the can or flat surface), and observe what happens. It should roll towards the balloon. Explain that this movement is caused by static electricity which was created by friction when you rubbed the balloon on your head
3 Now show children how to use static electricity to create a moving piece of art. Show children a butterfly made by sticking a cardboard body onto tissue paper wings (see Figure 8.3). Place it on a table and charge the balloon again, by rubbing it on your hair. Place the balloon over the wings and the tissue paper will move towards it, making it look like the butterfly is flying
4 Challenge children to create their own animal or scene that can be animated in the same way. Encourage them to create their own static electricity and test their creations. Do they move as intended?

4–7 years – children make a butterfly or bird. They make observations about how and why the wings move

7–9 years – children design their own static art. They make observations about how and why the parts move and offer scientific reasons for what they see

9–11 years – children design their own static art with multiple moving parts. They make observations about how and why the parts move and explain using terms such as *static energy* and *friction*

Key questions

● Does the moving part look effective?
● Could you have more than one moving part?
● Why does the balloon cause the tissue paper to move?

Helpful hints

● Note: static electricity is an imbalance of electrical charges – lightning is an example of static electricity

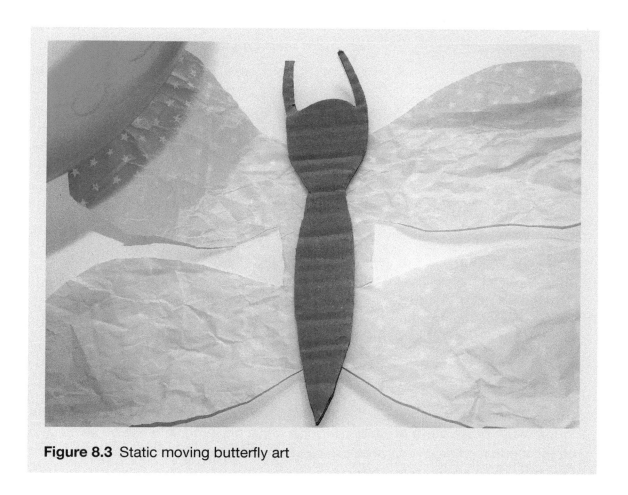

Figure 8.3 Static moving butterfly art

Prep for next week (bug-bots)

You will need to buy and prep toothbrush heads for next week

Session four
Bug-bots

This week, children are moving into the world of robotics, investigating how electrical circuits can be used to create fun, moving toys. They will build their own bug-bots from toothbrush heads, motors and small batteries, before pitting them against each other in bug-bot races.

Resources needed

Toothbrush heads (snap the tops off and cover any sharp edges with masking tape); small circular batteries; small motors; sticky pads; connecting wires; paper; card

Activity

1   Show children the bug-bot in Figure 8.4 and ask them how they think such a mini robot is made. Do the children think they would be able to make a moving bug-bot from the resources available to them? See if children can come up with some ideas

2   Model how to make a bug-bot by attaching a motor to one end of the toothbrush head using a sticky pad, then attach the circular battery to the other end of the toothbrush head using a second sticky pad (see Figure 8.5). The smaller the motor the better as a heavy motor weighs the bug down – circular flat motors are the best

3   Connect the wires to complete the circuit and the motor should vibrate, causing the toothbrush head to move. If it falls over, check that the motor and battery are central on the toothbrush head – children can pull them off and reattach them

4   Children have a go at making their own bug-bot. They can then go head to head with one another's bug-bots in races

   4–7 years – children make a bug-bot, then race against each other along the table-top. They make observations about what they see happening

   7–9 years – children construct a racing track out of paper and card for the bots to race along. They make observations and use terms like *cell*, *circuit* and *vibration* to describe how the bug-bot works

   9–11 years – children make changes to the basic design to try and improve their bug-bot. They use terms like *cell*, *circuit* and *vibration* to describe how the bug-bot works. Children investigate using more than one cell in their circuit

Key questions

● How does your bug-bot work?
● What would happen if you added another cell?

Helpful hints

- Note: the motor's vibrations cause the bot to move around. More cells may make the vibrations greater, which in turn will cause the bug-bot to move more aggressively
- Remind children to keep batteries away from mouths as they are very dangerous if swallowed

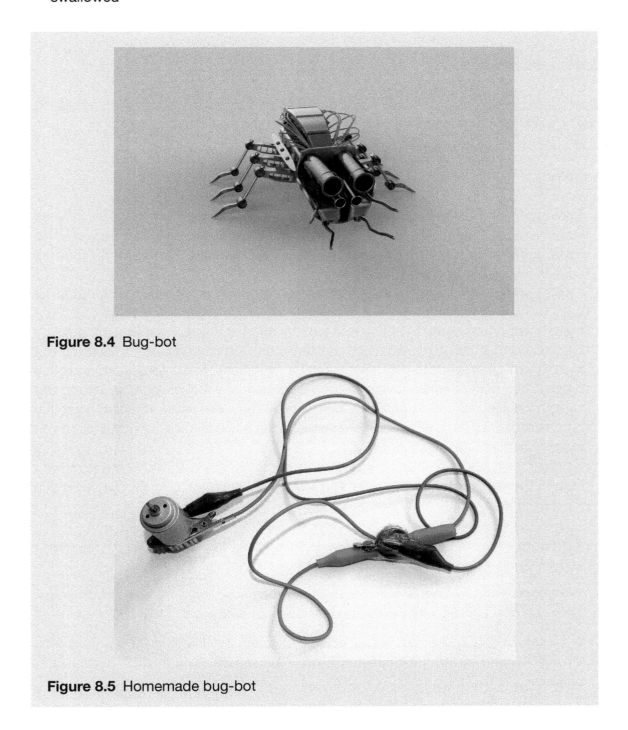

Figure 8.4 Bug-bot

Figure 8.5 Homemade bug-bot

Prep for next week (buzzers and bulbs)

Ask if any children have the game 'Operation,' or a similar game, that they could bring in

Session five
Buzzers and bulbs

Electricity is put to another fun use in this week's session, as children use the classic board-game 'Operation' to inspire their own buzzing, flashing wiggly wire challenge creations.

Resources needed

'Operation' game; electricity kits, including bulbs and buzzers; copper wire, modelling clay or old plastic containers

Activity

1 Show children the 'Operation' game and choose a couple of them to have a go. Ask why the buzzer sounds if the sides are touched. Explain that if the handle and sides meet, a complete circuit is formed, meaning that electricity is able to flow, which causes the buzzer to sound
2 Challenge children in teams of three to make a simple series circuit with a buzzer or bulb, using electrical kits. Younger children will likely be unfamiliar with this, so show them how to make a series circuit and then let them have a go themselves
3 Once the circuit has been made, ask children to find a suitable place to create a break in it. They then use crocodile clips to attach two 'loose' wires to either side of the break. Children then make a loop of copper wire and a wiggly copper structure, and using more crocodile clips, attach each to one of the loose wires. Children place the loop over the copper structure before securing the end with modelling clay or into an old plastic container (see Figure 8.6)
4 Children then test out their wire challenge game by trying to move the wire loop around the wiggly structure without the buzzer or light coming to life. Children can try out different wiggly structures to change the level of difficulty

   4–7 years – children make simple observations about the construction of the circuit and when the buzzer or bulb are activated

   7–9 years – children make a series circuit and can explain how and why it works. They can also explain why the buzzer and bulb are activated

   9–11 years – children make use of scientific vocabulary like *current* and *power* as they set up and explain their circuit. Children investigate using multiple buzzers and batteries

Key questions

● Why does the buzzer go off when you touch the wire?
● How does the circuit work?

Helpful hints

● Note: the buzzer sounds because the circuit is completed by the handle touching the wire

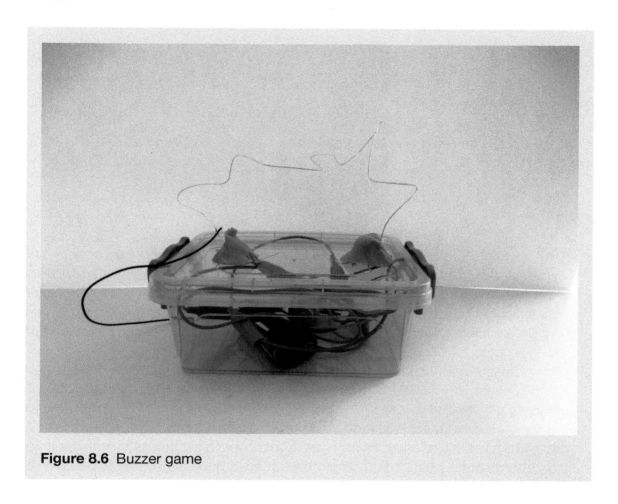

Figure 8.6 Buzzer game

Prep for next week (graphite circuits)

Make sure that you have true graphite pencils available for the next session

Session six
Graphite circuits

Building from Sessions four and five, where children created circuits using conventional materials, this week children will create a rather more unconventional circuit using lines drawn on paper.

Resources needed

Graphite pencils (one sharpened at both ends); 9-volt batteries in cases; LEDs; sticky tape; plain paper

Activity

1 Ask the children if they think they could light an LED with a pencil. How about if they just used part of it? Ask children which part of the pencil they write with (the lead), and if they know what it is made from. Explain that it is made from graphite, which is a material that conducts electricity. Have a pencil sharpened at both ends and connect the pencil, using crocodile clips, to a simple series circuit with a bulb. The bulb will light up
2 Draw a square onto paper, with two 1-centimetre gaps left on parallel sides – these are to connect your battery and bulb. Make sure that the lines are thick and that you are using a true graphite pencil. Place the 9-volt battery on one of the gaps ensuring the connectors are touching the separate pencil lines. Place the bulb across the other gap and secure in place with sticky tape, again ensuring the connectors are touching the pencil lines (see Figure 8.7). When the battery is in contact with the pencil lines, the bulb should light up. If it doesn't, the bulb wires may be attached to the pencil lines the wrong way around
3 Children experiment making their own graphite circuits – encourage them to be creative with the shapes they make. They could make a head shape, a flower shape or a wiggly pattern

4–7 years – children use the example shown to create their own graphite circuit. They make observations and describe what they see

7–9 years – children experiment with different images and sizes of graphite circuit. They offer scientific reasons for why their circuit works and equate the graphite lines with wire

9–11 years – children experiment with changing the length of the graphite lines, and test how thin the line can be before the circuit stops working. They report on their findings

Key questions

● What are the graphite lines taking the place of in a conventional circuit?
● Does the length of the line affect the brightness of the bulb?

Helpful hints

- Note: graphite is an electrical conductor – it allows power to travel around the image
- Note: longer lines or wires result in greater resistance causing a lower electricity flow

Figure 8.7 Graphite circuit

Prep for next time

Have a look through and decide which topic you will do next time – the introduction page of each chapter will tell you what you need to prep

9 Weather station

Over the course of this block, children will learn about some of the ways to measure and predict the weather. To help them with this, each week they will create a different scientific instrument to allow them to chart a specific aspect of the weather. In Session six, their challenge will be to create a UV shelter.

This block includes the following sessions (key resources underneath):

1 **Windsock**
   Range of materials for windsock: plastic bags, fabrics, paper; duct tape; sticky tape; masking tape; glue sticks; staplers; string; sticks
2 **Anemometer**
   Example anemometer; paper cups; pencils with rubbers on the top; straws; pins; scissors; sticky tape; modelling clay
3 **Rain gauge**
   Sample rain gauge; empty plastic bottles; masking tape; scissors; permanent markers; tape measures
4 **Thermometer**
   Thermometer; empty bottles; food colouring; clear straws; modelling clay; trays; ice; hot water; warm water; white card strips; masking tape; pens
5 **Barometer**
   Empty glass jars; balloons; rubber bands; glue; sticky tape; plastic straws; card measuring 4 cm × 6 cm; rulers; scissors; pencils
6 **UV lights**
   UV beads; four plastic food bags; three types of sunscreen with differing SPFs; lolly sticks; glue; sticky tape; blue tac; cardboard; newspaper; paper; fabric; pipe cleaners; scissors

In preparation for this block, try to find some real weather-monitoring equipment to show children. Note as well that you will need a wind source in Sessions one and two. If it happens to be a blustery day, fantastic; but if not, an electric fan will do. Session six requires UV light, so this session is best done on a clear and sunny day (it doesn't have to be a summer day, however). You will also need UV beads for this last session, which you may need to order in advance.

Session one
Windsock

We start this block with a windy challenge. Children will be creating their own windsock to measure the strength and direction of the wind (but not its speed). For the best results, take the windsocks outside on a windy day to test them out.

Resources needed

Range of materials for windsock: plastic bags, fabrics, paper; duct tape; sticky tape; masking tape; glue sticks; staplers; string; sticks

Activity

1 Show children Figure 9.1 and ask if they know what it is and how and where it is used. Explain that it is a windsock that measures the strength and direction of the wind. Highlight that it does not measure the speed of the wind – that is measured by an anemometer, which you will explore in Session two. How do children think a windsock works? It blows in the opposite direction from the wind. It is limp if the wind is weak and fully horizontal if the wind is strong

2 Do children have any ideas how they could make a windsock? They need to create a cylindrical shape that will move in the wind, so it needs to be flexible. Show children an array of fabrics, plastic bags and paper, as well as glue, various tapes and staplers. Challenge them to select a material and binding technique that they think will make a good windsock. Highlight the importance of the anchoring strings that attach it to a 'pole' to enable it to work. Children can use a stick as a pole

3 Children create their own windsocks, then take them outside to test. Was one material more popular than another? Was one material better than another? How have the children joined the material together to make their windsock? How have they attached a handle?

4–7 years – children make a simple windsock using their chosen material and glue or tape. They may need help attaching the anchoring strings

7–9 years – children make a windsock using their chosen material and glue, tape or staples. Challenge them to consider other useful properties for the material used, beyond being flexible (waterproof, bright in colour, etc.)

9–11 years – children can investigate which type of material or binding technique would be the most effective for a windsock. They can work in teams and try out a range of options and test them

Key questions

● Which was the most effective material, and why?
● How can you tell which direction the wind is coming from?

Helpful hints

- Note: wind direction is named for where it is coming from, not where it is going
- Note: windsocks are also used in chemical plants to show if there is a gas leak

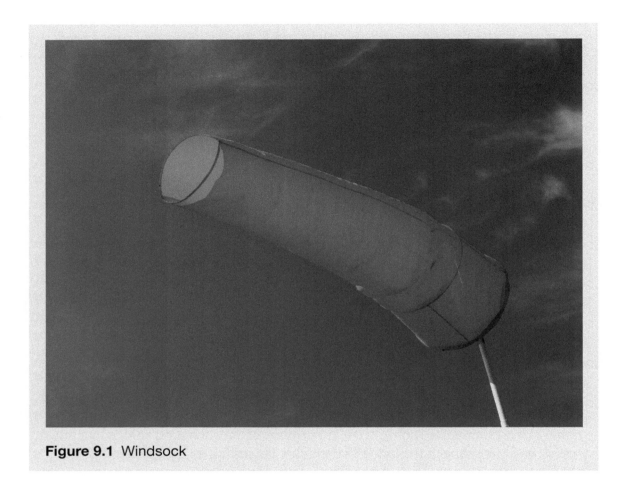

Figure 9.1 Windsock

Prep for next session (anemometer)

Prep a sample anemometer for the next session – see session notes for instructions

Session two
Anemometer

Today, we have a need for speed as children make an anemometer – their version will tell the how fast the wind is travelling by the speed of cups, unlike technical anemometers which have sensors inside to calculate the actual speed.

Resources needed

Sample anemometer; paper cups; pencils with rubbers on the top; straws; pins; scissors; sticky tape; modelling clay

Activity

1 Show children Figure 9.2 and ask if they know what it is and what it is measuring. Note that the cups move round when the wind blows – and that the faster they move, the greater the wind speed. This is an anemometer. Explain that most technical anemometers have a sensor inside that measures the actual wind speed

2 Model how to create an anemometer by taking one base paper cup and making four holes evenly spaced around the outside. Also make one hole in the bottom of the cup. Next, thread a straw through two of the holes that lie opposite each other, then repeat with the other two holes. There should be a cross formation made with the two straws

3 Attach a cup to the end of each straw by positioning the straw on the top of the cup with sticky tape (see Figure 9.3)

4 Finally, thread a pencil through the main base cup, ensuring the rubber sits underneath the cross made by the two straws. Secure with a pin and stabilise the anemometer by placing the end of the pencil in a paper cup with modelling clay inside

5 Children make their own anemometer then take them outside to test

4–7 years – children describe the mechanics of their anemometer and measure wind using the terms fast, moderate or gentle

7–9 years – children describe the mechanics of their anemometer and measure wind using the terms fast, moderate or gentle. They suggest possible modifications that might make their anemometer more accurate

9–11 years – children describe the mechanics of their anemometer using scientific terms including *force* and *wind resistance*. They measure wind speed using the terms fast, moderate, gentle and calm, and count turns per minute by tagging one of their cups with a marker pen. Children suggest possible modifications to make their anemometer more accurate

Key questions

● How will you distinguish between fast and moderate wind speed?
● Where would be a good place for an anemometer so that it measures true wind speed?

Helpful hints

● Note: cup anemometers count revolutions per minute to calculate wind speed

Figure 9.2 Anemometer

Figure 9.3 Anemometer

Prep for next session (rain gauge)

Ask children to find the annual rainfall figures for ten different countries around the world

Session three
Rain gauge

From windy to wet this week, as children create a rain gauge to measure just how much rainfall we get. You could even challenge children to record rainfall over a period of time and compare it to the national average at www.statista.com.

Resources needed

Sample rain gauge; empty plastic bottles; masking tape; scissors; permanent markers; tape measures

Activity

1   Look at Figure 9.4 and ask children what weather is forecast. Note the rain clouds, and ask children how they think we measure rainfall. Take ideas – hopefully the suggestion of 'collect it in a container' will come up. Explain that rainfall is collected in special collecting pots called rain gauges and is measured in millimetres (see Figure 9.5). Note that today, children will be measuring in centimetres, as it is easier to draw accurately

2   Ask children how they think they could make their own rain gauge from a plastic bottle. Take ideas and encourage them to come up with a design

3   Children cut off the top third of the bottle, turn it upside down and place it in to the remaining based of the bottle. Then challenge them to create a built-in measure on the bottle base with permanent marker. They mark in centimetres from the base of the bottle upwards (see Figure 9.6)

4   They test out their rain gauges using watering cans, then leave in a suitable place outside and wait for rain!

4–7 years – children make a rain gauge with plastic bottles already cut for them. They mark centimetres on the bottle using a tape measure to help them

7–9 years – children make a rain gauge independently. They mark centimetres on the bottle using a tape measure to help them

9–11 years – children make a rain gauge independently. They mark millimetres on the bottle using a tape measure to help them

Key questions

●   Where is the best place for the rain gauge outdoors?
●   Which months of the year do you think will have the greatest rainfall?

Helpful hints

●   Note: a modern version of a rain gauge is a seesaw design whereby drops of rain fall into either side into a jar. It determines amount of rain and how fast it is falling

Figure 9.4 Weather forecast

Figure 9.5 Weather station Rain gauge

Figure 9.6 Rain gauge

Prep for next session (thermometer)

Challenge children to find the highest and lowest temperatures ever recorded in your local area

Session four
Thermometer

Children have measured the wind and rain, but we still don't know if we are having balmy monsoons or freezing blizzards! Today, children are going to create their own thermometer and calibrate it to 'hot,' 'warm' and 'cold.'

Resources needed

Thermometer; empty bottles; food colouring; clear straws; modelling clay; trays; ice; hot water; warm water; white card strips; masking tape; pens

Activity

1 Ask children if they managed to find record highs and lows for your local area. How is this temperature measured? It can be recorded in two ways: Celsius or Fahrenheit. Note that a range of thermometers are used to measure temperature in weather stations, often relying on electrical resistance or an electromagnetic force to register the temperature. Explain that children will have a go today at creating a thermo-reader that measures variations in temperature, but will not actually give a reading

2 Model how to create a thermo-reader. Fill a bottle to the top with room-temperature water and add ten drops of food colouring to make it easier to see the liquid. Place a clear straw in the bottle, secured in place with modelling clay (see Figure 9.7). Ensure the straw is in the middle of the bottle top, and that there is no gap in the clay seal

3 Stick a strip of card behind the straw and put the bottle in a tray of hot water. Note that the water rises up the straw. Mark on the card where the line reached. Do children have any ideas about what has happened? Explain that the sudden rise in temperature causes particles in the water to separate out further, causing it to expand. Now put it in a tray of ice. What will happen this time? A drop in temperature causes particles to clump together, causing it to condense and move down. Mark this level on the card, too

4 Children make a thermometer and calibrate it to cold, warm and hot temperatures

4–7 years – children mark two different temperatures on the side of the bottle by placing in ice and marking where the line goes, then repeating this in warm water

7–9 years – children mark three or four different temperatures on the side of the bottle by placing in ice, cool water, tepid water and warm water

9–11 years – children calibrate their thermo-reader by placing it in different temperatures: ice, cool water, tepid water, warm water and hot water, marking where the line goes each time. They calibrate it with a thermometer by taking the temperature of each condition and noting this on the marked straw line

Key questions

● How accurate do you think the thermo-reader is?

Helpful hints

● Note: this thermometer indicates temperature change rather than measuring it

Figure 9.7 Thermometer

Prep for next session (barometer)

Ask children to bring in an empty glass jar for the next session

Session five
Barometer

Predicting the weather by how a straw moves up and down sounds like a trick a magician uses, but actually it is the way our homemade barometer works in this experiment. Once made, the children will be able to chart general weather conditions.

Resources needed

Empty glass jars; balloons; rubber bands; glue; sticky tape; plastic straws; card measuring 4 cm × 6 cm; rulers; scissors; pencils

Activity

1 Share any images of barometers that children have found, and discuss what they think it does. Explain that it shows changes in atmospheric pressure, which in turn tells us what weather to expect. Explain that children will make their own barometer today

2 Model making a barometer by cutting the neck off a balloon then stretching the remaining 'bulb' over the top of a glass jar. Secure it in place with a rubber band, making sure there are no gaps, or the barometer will not work correctly. Attach a one end of a straw to the top of the balloon with sticky tape, leaving the rest sticking out horizontally. The straw moves according to atmospheric pressure

3 On the card, draw a vertical line and label with a sun at the top and a rain cloud at the bottom. Secure this with modelling clay and stand near to the end of the straw sticking out away from the jar. Explain that low pressure usually causes rainy weather, while high pressure causes milder weather. Note that the pressure inside the jar doesn't change, but the pressure outside it does, which causes the pressure on the balloon to increase or decrease, which moves the straw. The straw's movement should indicate this on the card

4 Children make their own barometer and create an indicating label

4–7 years – children make barometer and label their card with a sun and rain cloud to show the change in pressure. The sun should be near the top and the rain cloud near the bottom

7–9 years – children make barometer and label their card with high and low pressure. High pressure should be near the top and low pressure near the bottom. They indicate the types of weather associated with each by drawing weather symbols next to them

9–11 years – children make barometer and label the piece of card with a scale marked in 1-centimetre increments. They write high pressure the top of the scale and low pressure at the bottom. Children draw associated weather symbols next to high and low

Key questions

● Which type of weather is predicted when it moves to high or low pressure?
● Where would be a good place to keep the barometer?

Helpful hints

- Note: the sun's heat, the seasons, altitude and latitude also affect air pressure

Figure 9.8 Barometer

Prep for next session (UV lights)

Children to research ways to stay safe in the sun. Also, order UV beads if you don't have any

Session six
UV lights

We end this block on a sunny high by investigating the power of ultraviolet (UV) light. Children use UV beads to investigate the effectiveness of sunscreen. They then create a UV bead animal and build an effective UV light busting shelter for it.

Resources needed

UV beads; four plastic food bags; three types of sunscreen with differing SPFs; lolly sticks; glue; sticky tape; blue tac; cardboard; newspaper; paper; fabric; pipe cleaners; scissors

Activity

1 Ask children to share as many ways to keep safe as they can in one minute. Discuss their ideas, paying particular attention to discussing the use of sunscreen – ascertain understanding of sun protection factor (SPF)
2 Show children the UV beads and explain that they react to UV light from the sun. Explain that you are going to carry out an experiment today to see how effective different sunscreens are at blocking the damaging UV rays from the sun. Ask children to suggest how we might do this
3 Discuss how you could put some beads in four different plastic food bags and on three of the bags rub a different type of sunscreen, then place all four bags in the direct sun. Why will they not put sunscreen on the fourth bag? It is the control to see what happens without sunscreen. Put the bags in direct sunlight and note after 15 minutes what has happened to the colour of the UV beads. Is there a correlation between the SPF rating on the sunscreen and its effectiveness at blocking UV light?
4 While the bead experiment is in the sun, challenge children to make a simple UV bead animal by threading beads onto a pipe cleaner. Challenge them make a shelter using any of the materials available to them that might protect their UV animals from the sun. Place in the sun and observe. Which material was most effective, and why?

4–7 years – children make observations about how effective their material and design is based on the colour of the UV animal beads

7–9 years – children make observations about how effective their material and design is based on the colour of the UV animal beads. They offer reasons for observations

9–11 years – children make observations about how effective their material and design is, using scientific language such as *radiation* and *sunrays*

Key questions

● Which material was the best at keeping the sunlight out?

Helpful hints

● Make sure that you use completely clear plastic bags so that the UV light is not blocked by branded images or writing that may appear on the bag

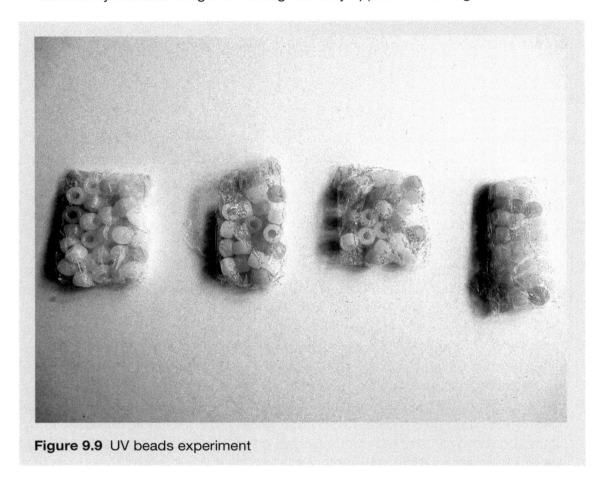

Figure 9.9 UV beads experiment

Prep for next session

Have a look through and decide which topic you will do next time – the introduction page of each chapter will tell you what you need to prep

10 The experimental kitchen

Over the course of this block, children will explore and experiment with everyday ingredients found in the kitchen. They will learn about the chemistry of baking, look at the way ingredients interact with each other and explore some non-culinary uses for foodstuffs. During the final session, children will get to make their own ice cream.

This block includes the following sessions (key resources underneath):

1 **Cake chemistry**
Cake ingredients: flour, sugar, oil, eggs, baking powder; mugs; forks; microwave; paper plates; pens

2 **Magic milk**
Block of butter (real or an image); double cream in jars that have been left out overnight; mugs of warm milk; plates or shallow bowls of milk; vinegar; food colouring; washing-up liquid; pipettes; digital cameras

3 **Electrical food**
Sample fruit circuit; lemons; limes; oranges; apples; carrots; potatoes; tomatoes; zinc coated nails; copper wire; pennies; light bulbs, buzzers or motors; voltmeter

4 **Cleaning food**
Items to clean with: vinegar, lemons, ketchup, salt, bicarbonate of soda, cream of tartar; water for mixing; items to clean: stained linen, mucky mirror, copper coins, stained wooden chopping board, ink-stained disposable cloths; trays

5 **Walking rainbow water**
Water; clear cups or glasses; thin kitchen towel; range of food colouring; Skittles™ (or other colour-coated, shelled sweets); china plates

6 **Ice adventures**
Two or three bottles of purified water that have been in the freezer for around 2 hours, 45 minutes – ice crystals should be beginning to form in the water; ice cubes; milk; sugar; vanilla essence; fruit juice; small and large zip-lock bags; salt; bowls; spoon

In preparation for each session in this block, gather together the ingredients needed. You will also need access to a microwave for Session one, some basic circuit equipment for Session three and a freezer for Session six.

Session one
Cake chemistry

Don't expect any of this week's cake creations to win any culinary prizes, as children tinker with the classic cake recipe to investigate the role each ingredient plays in the science of baking.

Resources needed

Cake ingredients: flour, sugar, oil, eggs, baking powder; mugs; forks; microwave; paper plates; pens

Activity

1 Ask children if they know what the key ingredients are for baking a cake. Make a list and add in any that are missing. Your list should include: flour, butter or oil, sugar, baking powder and eggs. What do children think each ingredient's role is?
2 Get children into groups of four and challenge them to create four cakes using the ingredients in Figure 10.1. Explain that the first cake should include all the ingredients, while the other three cakes should each have a different ingredient missing: the eggs, the baking powder or the oil. Children mix the ingredients together in a mug and cook them in a microwave for two minutes at a time
3 Once cooked, help children scoop the cakes out of their mugs (it will be very hot) and place on paper plates. Write on the plate which ingredient has been left out
4 Children taste the cakes and decide what they think the role of each ingredient is in the cooking process. They rank their cakes based on taste, texture and appearance
5 Children share their findings. Explain that the baking powder reacts to produce carbon dioxide gas which helps create air in the cake; the egg creates strong structures in the cake because it contains proteins which reform when cooked, making the cake hold together; and the oil coats other ingredients to keep the cake moist

   4–7 years – children describe the taste, texture and look of each cake. They describe what is 'wrong' with each cake

   7–9 years – children describe the taste, texture and look of each cake. They suggest the role of the missing ingredient in terms of the changes during cooking and the final cakes

   9–11 years – children describe the taste, texture and look of each cake. They suggest the role of the missing ingredient in scientific terms noting changes that happen when heated

Key questions

● What is wrong with the cake texture, flavour and appearance without this ingredient?

Helpful hints

- Make sure that children know which cake is in which mug before they cook them

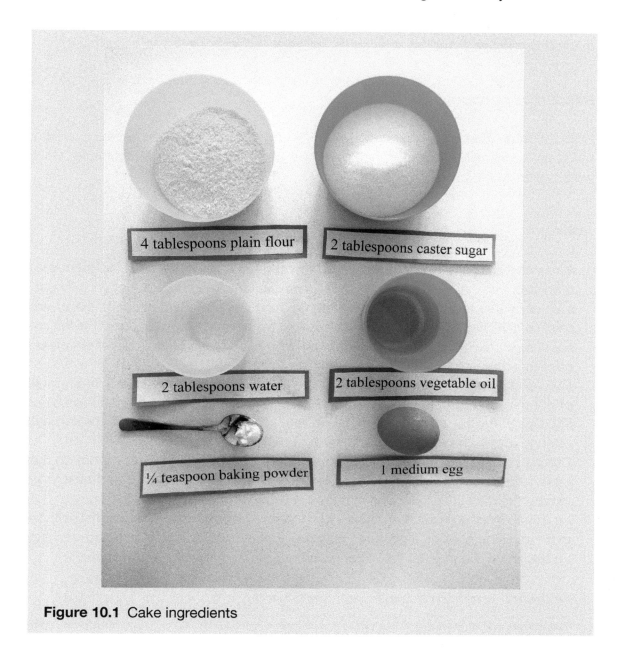

Figure 10.1 Cake ingredients

Prep for next session (magic milk)

Leave out some double cream in jars overnight before the next session

Session two
Magic milk

Today, children will investigate how we make butter from cream and will explore other magical properties of milk as they make 'milk art' and 'milk plastic.'

Resources needed

Block of butter (real or an image); double cream in jars that have been left out overnight; mugs of warm milk; plates or shallow bowls of milk; vinegar; food colouring; sieve; washing-up liquid; pipettes; digital cameras

Activity

1   Show children a block of butter and ask them where it comes from. Establish that is a dairy product, so comes from cream or milk. Get children into groups and give each a jar of double cream that has been left out overnight. Tell them to shake the jar until the feel of it changes and they notice a solid lump forming – this is butter. The leftover liquid is buttermilk. The butter should be yellow in colour. Explain that the children have just churned their own butter

2   Now explain that children are going to create plastic from milk. Give children mugs of hot milk and get them to add two tablespoons of vinegar and some food colouring. Observe what happens. Once the milk has separated, children pour the contents through a sieve and scoop out the hard 'plastic' left behind

3   Children can play with their 'plastic' and mould it into different things. What do they think has happened? Explain that the vinegar reacts with the milk and essentially 'grabs' the molecules, creating clumps of rubbery material

4   As a final exploration of 'magic milk,' give children a shallow bowl or plate of milk. Let them experiment using pipettes to put small amounts of food colouring and washing-up liquid into the milk. Children can photograph the effects to create milk art

4–7 years – children describe what they observe

7–9 years – children describe what they observe. They make suggestions as to what might be happening

9–11 years – children describe what they observe using scientific terms such as: *colloid, reaction, molecules, fats* and *proteins*

Key questions

● Do you think you could turn the butter back into cream?
● Why does the milk separate out?
● Why do you think the colours seem to move?

Helpful hints

- Note: shaking the cream causes fat globules to separate out and form butter
- Note: liquid soap affects the surface tension of milk, causing its molecules to go wild!

Figure 10.2 Making butter

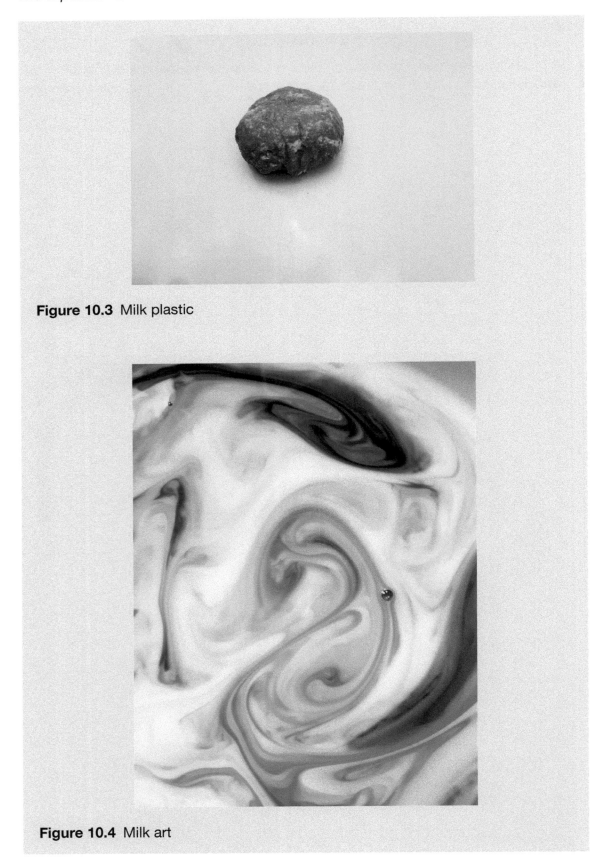

Figure 10.3 Milk plastic

Figure 10.4 Milk art

Prep for next session (electrical food)

Do a trial run of electrical fruit before the next session so that you have an example to show

Session three
Electrical food

This week's session is going to be electric, hopefully, as children investigate which foods can light up a bulb.

Resources needed

Example fruit circuit; lemons; limes; oranges; apples; carrots; potatoes; tomatoes; zinc coated nails; copper wire; pennies; light bulbs, buzzers or motors; voltmeter

Activity

1 Show children a range of fruits and vegetables, and a light bulb. Do they think any of the food items be used as a battery to light up the bulb? Explain that today children are going to set up an experiment to find out

2 Show children your example, then model how to set up the experiment (see Figure 10.5). Cut a penny-sized incision into a potato. Take two pieces of copper wire and wrap the end of one around a penny and the end of the other around a nail. Press the penny into the slit in the potato and push the nail in on the opposite side, ensuring in both cases that the end of the wire is sticking out. Connect the copper wires to each side of your bulb, buzzer or motor and watch what happens

3 Working in groups, encourage children to experiment with all of the different fruits and vegetables. They should log their findings. What conclusions can they drawn? Which fruit and vegetables have they identified as generating electricity? Explain that they contain acid which reacts with the metals creating a current that flows from one electrode (the zinc nail) to the other (the penny)

4–7 years – children create their circuits with support. They describe what they see

7–9 years – children create their own circuits and describe how a circuit works

9–11 years – children create their own circuits and describe how a circuit works. They also experiment with buzzers and motors. Children use a voltmeter to measure how much electricity is generated

Key questions

● How do you know that it is generating electricity?
● Which other fruit and veg do you think might generate electricity?

Helpful hints

● The more acidic a fruit is, the higher the electrical generation
● ***Do not*** eat the fruits or vegetables used in these experiments

- Note: the voltage is created by a chemical reaction between the metals and the acid in the fruit or vegetable. This reaction causes a flow of electrons from the negative electrode (zinc nail) to the positive electrode (penny)

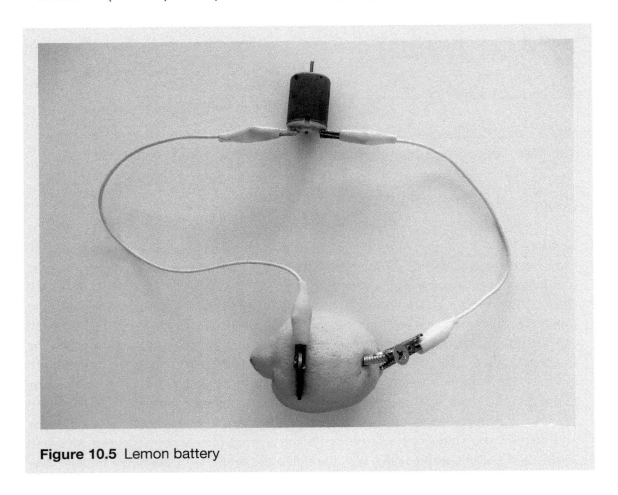

Figure 10.5 Lemon battery

Prep for next session (cleaning foods)

Prepare your 'dirty' items for next session in advance

Session four
Cleaning food

We all know from experience just how messy food can be, but what if it could also be used to help with the household cleaning? In this session, children are going to experiment with a range of kitchen ingredients to discover which can do just that.

Resources needed

Items to clean with: vinegar, lemons, ketchup, salt, bicarbonate of soda, cream of tartar; water for mixing; items to clean: stained linen, mucky mirror, copper coins, stained wooden chopping board, ink-stained disposable cloths; trays

Activity

1 Show children the items you have that require cleaning and the food products you have with which to clean them. What do they think? Can they clean the objects, or will the foodstuffs simply make them even dirtier?
2 Let children experiment in pairs with the food and the objects, encouraging them to investigate in a logical manner. Give them cotton wool balls to use as cleaning 'cloths' and suggest that they only use a small amount of each foodstuff. Explain that they can mix things with water to create a paste or watered-down liquid. Children should experiment on trays
3 Children record their findings, indicating if they were successful or not, and try to give reasons. They may find that more than one thing works on any given object. Note that it is generally the chemical reactions caused that make certain items effective cleaners
4 Now challenge children to find a cleaning solution for an ink-stained cloth. This will need a mixture of two items to clean it. Suggest they try: tartar and lemon juice (this one should work); salt and lemon juice; bicarbonate of soda and lemon juice (this will react a lot). Ensure children mix small amounts and experiment on trays

4–7 years – children record findings and describe what they observe

7–9 years – children record findings and suggest what might be happening

9–11 years – children record findings and suggest what might be happening using scientific terms such as *acidic*, *abrasion* and *reaction*

Key questions

● Why did you not try the ketchup on the cloth?
● What do you think has happened to the grime?
● What else do you think this might clean?

Helpful hints

- Note: vinegar cleans the mirror; lemon juice or bicarbonate of soda will clean the stained linen; ketchup cleans the coins; salt cleans the chopping board; cream of tartar followed by some lemon juice clean the ink-stained cloths

Figure 10.6 Kitchen ingredient cleaning products

Prep for next session (walking rainbow water)

Ask children to bring in an empty plastic 1-litre bottle for the next session

Session five
Walking rainbow water

Today, children are going to create both walking rainbow water and a plate of rainbow water, using two different scientific phenomena. These experiments are not only scientifically fascinating, but also create beautiful effects.

Resources needed

Water; clear cups or glasses; thin kitchen towel; range of food colouring; Skittles (or other colour-coated, shelled sweets); china plates

Activity

1 Can children tell you the colours of the rainbow? Have they ever encountered such colours in food? They may have seen a rainbow cake, for example (see Figure 10.7)
2 Explain that children are going to first experiment with rainbow colour-coated shelled sweets set around the outside of a plate. Get children to set this up and add a thin layer of water to the plate so that the sweets are just sitting in it, and leave. Ask children to predict what will happen
3 While the first experiment is developing, children embark on creating walking rainbow water. They lay out eight glasses or clear cups and fill alternate cups with 100 ml of coloured water (see Figure 10.8). Then they place a piece of folded kitchen towel between each glass and observe (see Figure 10.9). Why do they think the water is 'walking' up the kitchen towel and into the adjacent glass or cup? The movement is due to capillary action
4 Children can now check on their sweet experiment and describe what has happened (see Figure 10.10). Note that the movement of the colouring is due to diffusion

4–7 years – children make observations

7–9 years – children make observations and give suggestions as to what might be happening

9–11 years – children make observations and give suggestions as to what might be happening using scientific language such as: *dissolve*, *diffusion* and *capillary action*

Key questions

● Why has the water moved?
● Why do the colours from the sweets spread into the water?

Helpful hints

● Note: capillary action moves the 'walking water' because the adhesive forces between the water and the kitchen towel are stronger than the cohesive forces in the water alone
● Note: colour from the sweets dissolves in the water and moves through it via diffusion

Figure 10.7 Rainbow cake

Figure 10.8 Walking rainbow water I

Figure 10.9 Walking rainbow water II

Figure 10.10 Coloured sweets experiment

Prep for next session (ice adventures)

Check with children for dairy or juice allergies for next time when they will make ice cream

Session six
Ice adventures

Today, children are going to make an icy treat, but they won't be using a freezer. Instead, they will explore the nature of ice and how temperature can be manipulated with just a pinch of salt.

Resources needed

Two or three bottles of purified water that have been in the freezer for around 2 hours, 45 minutes – ice crystals should be beginning to form in the water; ice cubes; milk; sugar; vanilla essence; fruit juice; small and large zip-lock bags; salt; bowls; spoons

Activity

1   Start the session by taking one of your bottles of ice-cold water and bashing it – the water should instantly turn to ice. Explain that the water freezes as it comes into contact with impurities or movement. This process is called nucleation
2   Now ask children if they know the freezing point of water – about 0°C or 32°F. What do they think happens if you add salt to ice? Try it – it will melt. Explain that the salt not only lowers the freezing point temperature to around −18°C or 0°F, but also makes the overall mixture colder than ice alone. Explain that children are going to test this out today as they make ice cream or a fruit slushy
3   Get children to put milk, sugar and vanilla essence (for ice cream) or just fruit juice (for a slushy), in a small zip-lock sandwich bag with the air squeezed out (see Figure 10.11). Then add ice and salt to a bigger zip-lock bag and place the smaller bag in the bigger bag and shake it around for a few minutes – the contents of the small bag should begin to freeze. If left long enough, it would freeze solid. Children remove the small bag, rinse it and put into a bowl to eat (see Figure 10.12)

    4–7 years – children follow guidance and make observations about the changing states

    7–9 years – children follow guidance and make observations about the changing states. They use the terms *freezing point*, *solid* and *liquid*

    9–11 years – children follow guidance and make observations about the changing states. They use the terms *freezing point*, *solid*, *liquid*, *nucleation* and *molecules*

Key questions

● What is happening to the water?
● Why has the ice and salt frozen the milk or juice?

Helpful hints

● Note: the milk and juice freeze because the temperature of the salt and ice mixture is colder than ice alone. The reason for this is complicated! When the ice starts to melt, this uses up energy which causes the overall temperature of the mixture to lower

Figure 10.11 Making ice cream I

Figure 10.12 Making ice cream II

Prep for next time

Have a look through and decide which topic you will do next time – the introduction page of each chapter will tell you what you need to prep

11 In the garden

Over the course of this block, children will care for seeds and plants, as well as consider how they can help nature and wildlife in their own locality. The activities are designed to be both fun and educational, with a view to enthusing children about the positive impact they can have on nature and wildlife. Children will plant or create something each session, setting up a garden space that can be enjoyed long after the block has finished.

This block includes the following sessions (key resources underneath):

1 **Growing plants**
   Time-lapse video of cress seeds growing (examples can be found online); cress seeds; paper plates; cotton wool; water; jug; plastic plant pots; soil; lolly sticks; sunflower seeds; variety of herb seeds

2 **Sprout house**
   Transparent plastic wallet; house template; cotton wool; empty glass jar; cocktail sticks; sponges in variety of colours and sizes; water; plates; scissors; variety of seeds (cress, chia, alfalfa seeds sprout quickly)

3 **Scarecrow design**
   Images of scarecrows; materials to make scarecrows: old pipes/tubes, plastic bags, newspapers, fabric, cotton wool, plant pots, string, straws, lolly sticks, buttons, sticks, marker pens, wire; sticky tape; PVA glue

4 **Making leaf compost**
   Transparent sandwich bags; 1-litre water bottles; glass jars; soil; sand; worms (gathered from outside); newspaper; variety of natural matter: dry and fresh leaves, bark, vegetable peelings

5 **Seed bombs and bird feeders**
   Powdered or air-drying clay; soil; water; wildflower seeds; empty plastic bottles; pencils; compasses; string; bird seed; card tubes; unsalted nut butter; knives; apples; sunflower seeds

6 **Bug hotels**
   A4 paper; pencils; wooden planks or crates; string; small plant pots; old bits of wood; dead leaves; bark; twigs; rocks; old bricks; nails; hammers

In preparation for each session, gather together the relevant resources, ensuring there is enough for all children. Session one requires a time-lapse video, which you should be able to find online.

Session one
Growing plants

Growing a plant from seed is always hugely satisfying, especially when a rapidly growing plant, like cress, is involved. Children will also be planting for the long haul, however, as they prepare, plant and nurture plants over a number of weeks.

Resources needed

Time-lapse video of cress seeds growing (find online); cress seeds; paper plates; cotton wool; water; jug; plastic plant pots; soil; lolly sticks; sunflower seeds; variety of herb seeds

Activity

1 Ask children if they have ever grown a plant. What did they grow, how did they plant it and care for it?
2 Show children the cress seeds, cotton wool and water. How do they think they could use these to grow something? Note that cress is a rapid growing plant. Show children a time-lapse video of cress seeds growing (examples can be found online)
3 Model how to make initials out of cotton wool and place onto a paper plate (see Figure 11.1). Water the cotton wool and add a layer of cress seeds on top. Children then create their own cotton wool initials and sow their cress. They water them daily
4 While cress is fast growing, other plants take a lot longer to grow, and as such need more care and attention. Explain that children are going to plant sunflower seeds and herb seeds and look after them over the course of the next six weeks
5 Model how to sow the seeds (see Figure 11.2). Fill a pot two-thirds of the way full of soil before placing the seeds on top and covering with more soil. Give the seeds a good water and label them with a lolly stick
6 Find a warm place for the seeds to germinate. Ensure that children water the seeds daily

4–7 years – children sow four or five sunflower seeds in one pot and some herbs in another. They note the care instructions in pictorial format

7–9 years – children sow several different herb seeds and sunflowers. They note down the care instructions for each

9–11 years – children sow several different herb seeds and sunflowers. They note down the care instructions for each and note what to expect

Key questions

- What conditions do you think a seed needs in order to germinate?
- Can you name any parts of a plant?

Helpful hints

- Note: different seeds will germinate at different rates
- Note: seeds need water, warmth and oxygen to germinate

Figure 11.1 Cress initials

Figure 11.2 Planting seeds

Prep for next session (sprout house)

Ensure children water their cress seeds every day before the next session

Session two
Sprout house

After their introduction to basic planting in the last session, children will take it up a notch this time as they plant a sprout house. They can watch their house take shape and literally grow over a number of days.

Resources needed

Transparent plastic wallet; house template; cotton wool; empty glass jar; cocktail sticks; sponges in a variety of colours and sizes; water; plates; scissors; variety of seeds (cress, chia, alfalfa seeds sprout quickly)

Activity

1 Children start by checking on their cress initials, which should have grown by now. Explain that they are going to plant some more fast-growing seeds today, but in the form of a more elaborate construction

2 Model how to make a sprout house using sponges and toothpicks (see Figure 11.3). Start by placing a large green sponge on a plate – this will form the grass base of the house – then add four smaller sponges to create the walls, connecting them to the grass using toothpicks. Once you are happy with the size and shape of the house, attach two more pieces of sponge to make the slanting roof, again using toothpicks

3 Children then make their own houses. Once complete, they dampen the sponges, mix the seeds with a little water (making them slightly sticky) and then sprinkle them onto the sponges, covering the grass and roof

4–7 years – children use pre-cut sponges. They use two types of seed

7–9 years – children use pre-cut sponges and try to incorporate a chimney. They use a variety of seeds

9–11 years – children cut their own sponges and incorporate a chimney. They create some arch-shaped walls. They use a variety of seeds, thinking about aesthetics

Key questions

● What conditions do seeds need to germinate?
● What do you expect to see when the seeds grow?

Helpful hints

● Note: once a seed has germinated, it is called a seedling
● Note: the parts of a seedling are root, shoot and leaves – children can try to spot these

Figure 11.3 Sprout house

Prep for next session (scarecrow design)

Find a suitable outdoor area for the seeds, with enough space to also accommodate the scarecrows that will be created in the next session

Session three
Scarecrow design

Scarecrows are traditionally used as a deterrent by farmers trying to stop birds from eating their crops. There are even a number of scarecrow festivals. Today, children will have a go at making their own scarecrow using a range of materials and a lot of imagination.

Resources needed

Images of scarecrows; materials to make scarecrows: old pipes/tubes, plastic bags, newspapers, fabric, cotton wool, plant pots, string, straws, lolly sticks, buttons, sticks, marker pens, wire; sticky tape; PVA glue

Activity

1 Show children images of scarecrows in Figures 11.4–11.7 and any others you have found. Can children explain the job of a scarecrow?
2 Ask them which design features they think might make a scarecrow successful. Note that bright colours, strange shapes, exaggerated features and gestures might all be effective at scaring birds. Note also that materials such as paper or card would not last very long if it rained. These can be your success criteria
3 Explain that, working in groups of three, children are going to have a go at making a scarecrow. These will be used to protect their seeds and plants from birds
4 Discuss how they might use the materials available to make a scarecrow. They could use a plant pot or a stuffed plastic bag for the head and/or body. They might use wool, string, or shredded fabric for hair, and create facial features from buttons or marker pens. Emphasise that the design is entirely up to them
5 Once complete, children can sit their scarecrows by their pots

4–7 years – children create a scarecrow that meets at least two of the success criteria

7–9 years – children create a scarecrow that meets at least three of the success criteria. Children use internal wire in the arms to create gestures

9–11 years – children create a scarecrow that meets at all of the success criteria. Children use an internal wire 'skeleton' to create gestures

Key questions

● Does your scarecrow meet the success criteria?
● How would you make a life-size scarecrow?
● Why do you think that scarecrows only work for a short period of time?

Helpful hints

● Note: a scarecrow is usually only effective for a short amount of time before the birds realise that it is not a real human
● Note: modern-day crop protection techniques include the use of an infrared sensor which emits an ultrasonic wave to scare birds and animals

Figure 11.4 Scarecrow

Figure 11.5 Scarecrow

Figure 11.6 Scarecrow

Figure 11.7 Scarecrow

Prep for next session (making leaf compost)

Ask children to bring in a 1-litre plastic bottle for next session

Session four
Making leaf compost

Although the decomposition process, integral to making compost, is somewhat lengthy (months or years), setting up the composter and setting the wheels in motion can be fun, too. Today, children will have a go at setting up a composter to make leaf compost, but make sure they wash their hands thoroughly afterwards and that they wear gloves when handling worms.

Resources needed

Transparent sandwich bags; 1-litre water bottles; glass jars; soil; sand; worms (gathered from outside); newspaper; variety of natural matter: dry and fresh leaves, bark, vegetable peelings

Activity

1 Remind children that seeds need water, warmth and oxygen to germinate. Once germinated, though, what do the seedlings need to grow into plants? Gather ideas and establish that water, light, oxygen, correct temperature and nutrients are all needed

2 Ask children how gardeners boost the nutrients in soil for plants. Note that compost is commonly used, as it gives goodness to the soil. Do children know what compost is made from? They may have a compost bin at home, or put food waste out for local collection. Explain that they are going to have a go today at creating leaf compost, which is a compost made from leaves and other garden materials

3 Head outside with children and gather some leaves and other suitable natural materials. Note that material found near roads or on the street may contain litter or pollution, so is best to avoid. Children should also collect soil to place in the bottom of their compost bottle

4 Model how to create compost using an empty cut-off bottle. Sort the materials that have been collected, along with any vegetable or fruit peelings, and then create layers of each material in the bottle (see Figure 11.8). Children then create their own composter filled with layers which they can take home and monitor to see if it eventually turns into compost. Note that it should be kept outside

   4–7 years – children create their leaf compost, identifying the various materials they have gathered. They can explain that compost produces nutrients for plants

   7–9 years – children create their leaf compost, identifying the various materials they have gathered. They explain the process and benefits of decomposition in simple terms

   9–11 years – children create a compost wormery by layering soil and sand in a glass jar, then watering it and adding a few worms (see Figure 11.9). They add a layer of fresh leaves or vegetable peelings, and cover the outside of the jar with newspaper. Children explain the process of decomposition in detail using scientific language

Key questions

- Why should you not use natural materials from the roadside?
- How long do you think it will take to break down?

Helpful hints

- Note: bacteria and fungi are true decomposers (saprophytes); worms are detritivores
- Note: man-made items are unsuitable for compost as they are less bio-degradable

Figure 11.8 Leaf compost bottle

Figure 11.9 Wormery compost

Prep for next session (seed bombs and bird feeders)

Ask children to research types of bird feeder that they might like to make in the next session

Session five
Seed bombs and bird feeders

Today, children will turn their attention to the occupants of the garden environment, as they entice and sustain bird and insect visitors by creating seed bombs and bird feeders.

Resources needed

Powdered or air-drying clay; soil; water; wildflower seeds; empty plastic bottles; pencils; compasses; string; bird seed; card tubes; unsalted nut butter; knives; apples; sunflower seeds

Activity

1   How do children think they can help encourage more pollinating insects and birds to visit garden areas to help increase the number of seeds, flowers and plants growing? Take suggestions, then explain that seed bombs encourage insects to visit, while bird feeders encourage our feathered friends into the garden

2   Model making a seed bomb: mix clay with compost and wildflower seeds. The ratio should be five parts clay to one part compost and one part seeds. Add water to form a sticky, dough-like consistency. Form into fist-sized shapes, and dry in a warm place

3   Children then make their own seed bombs. When dry, they can use them in a suitable outdoor area, or alternatively take them home. To use the bombs, throw them in a suitable outdoors position, such as an unused flower bed or underneath a tree

4   Now show children three options for making a bird feeder. The first is a simple tube feeder which uses a cardboard tube and a loop of string threaded through for a handle. The tube is coated with nut butter then rolled in bird seed (see Figure 11.10)

5   The second option is an apple feeder. Core an apple and loop a piece of wool through to create a handle. Children then press sunflower seeds into the flesh of the apple, covering it completely (see Figure 11.11)

6   For the third option, children pierce a pencil horizontally all the way through an empty bottle. This will be a perch for the birds. Repeat this with a second pencil, this time at a 90° angle to the first. Pierce holes around the bottle using a compass point so that birds can access the seeds. Attach string to the bottle neck for a handle and fill with bird seed mix (see Figure 11.12). Feeders should be hung in a suitable outdoor area

4–7 years – children create one of the simple bird feeders

7–9 years – children choose which feeder to make

9–11 years – children make two different feeders

Key questions

● Why are seeds and fats good for birds?

Helpful hints

● Note: check if there are any children with nut allergies before using nut butter

Figure 11.10 Tube bird feeder

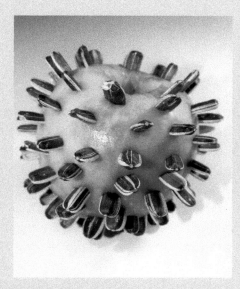

Figure 11.11 Apple bird feeder

Figure 11.12 Bottle bird feeder

Prep for next session (bug hotels)

Try to source wooden crates and planks for the next session. Find suitable bug hotel locations

Session six
Bug hotels

After the seed bombs and bird feeders of Session five, this session children will create an inviting, five-star bug hotel for our creepy, crawly little friends.

Resources needed

A4 paper; pencils; wooden planks or crates; string; small plant pots; old bits of wood; dead leaves; bark; twigs; sticks; rocks; old bricks; nails; hammers

Activity

1 Discuss what a minibeast is, and the important role they have within our ecosystem. Which minibeasts would the children be likely to see if they walked around the local area? Take the children for a bug hunt and record the insects seen. As the children carry out the hunt, get them to gather materials suitable for the interior of a bug hotel (dead leaves, bark, twigs, sticks, pine cones, rocks, old bricks)
2 Explain that children are going to make a bug hotel, both to encourage the existing bugs to stay in the area and to help the population grow
3 Explore the materials available to structure and fill the bug hotel. Discuss how to build up layers of different materials to create compartments. Each compartment should have a different type of material in order to encourage a range of insects. Twigs also need to be placed with their ends facing outwards, so insects can burrow in the small gaps
4 Divide children into two teams, providing each with a wooden crate or a number of planks. Challenge them to create their own bug hotels in situ – show them Figures 11.13–11.16 for further ideas

   4–7 years – children focus on the content and overall structure. They incorporate four main compartments, making sure there are gaps for insects

   7–9 years – children focus on the content, overall structure and the types of bug they want to attract. They incorporate at least six compartments, making sure there are gaps for insects

   9–11 years – children focus on the content, overall structure and the types of bug they want to attract. They incorporate multiple, well-designed compartments that incorporate a range of sizes of gaps

Key questions

- Which insects do you think will live there?
- Where will you position your bug hotel?

Helpful hints

- Note: insect populations are declining partly due to urbanisation and use of pesticides
- Note: a large drop in insect populations would devastate most ecosystems

Figure 11.13 Bug hotel

Figure 11.14 Bug hotel

Figure 11.15 Bug hotel

Figure 11.16 Bug hotel

Prep for next time

Have a look through and decide which topic you will do next time – the introduction page of each chapter will tell you what you need to prep

12 Wild races

Over the course of this block, children will face an array of transport-related challenges from soap-powered boats to cotton reel cars and flying machines. Children will consider the forces at work as they load, test and race their vehicles.

1 **Balloon car race**

Empty water bottles or small boxes; screw lids; wooden dowels, skewers or pencils; sticky tape; scissors; elastic bands; balloons; old CDs; thick card; modelling clay

2 **Cotton reel car race**

Cotton reel car made without the washer; cotton reels; burnt/used matchsticks or chopped skewers; elastic bands; pencils; flat washers; pencil alternatives: straws, nails, skewers; matchstick alternatives: paper clips, pipe cleaners

3 **Power boat race**

Aluminium foil; foil trays; card; cardboard boxes; paper; empty water bottles; cotton reels; elastic bands; burnt/used matches; flat washers; duct tape; masking tape; sticky tape; lolly sticks; pencils; straws; corks; a water tray or piping

4 **Soap boat race**

Water; rice cereal; washing-up liquid; thick card; scissors; PVA glue; liquid hand soap; hand cleaning gel; cotton buds; a water tray or piping

5 **Parachute slow race**

Plastic bin bags; string or wool; Lego people; scissors; sticky tape; yoghurt pots

6 **Flying saucers**

Frisbee™; paper plates (two sizes); sticky tape; scissors; felt tip pens

In preparation for this block, create a league table for teams to record their successes in each race. You will also need to consider where you will complete races. Although the key components for each session are listed here, you may want to have a wider variety of material available for children to choose from.

Session one
Balloon car race

Event one in the Wild Race Series is balloon car racing. Children will design vehicles that can be powered by inflated balloons, before pitting them against one another for a place on the leader board.

Resources needed

Empty water bottles or small boxes; screw lids; wooden dowels, skewers or pencils; sticky tape; scissors; elastic bands; balloons; old CDs; thick card; modelling clay

Activity

1 Explain that each session in this block will see children design a vehicle to race. Today they will be making balloon-powered cars. Show them Figures 12.1 and 12.2, and ask them to discuss with a partner how each has been made and how they move
2 Children share ideas. Clarify that the balloon is blown up to make the car move. It is the release of the balloon and the air shooting out which causes the movement. Note that the axles need to rotate freely to enable the car to go – children use cut straws and skewers for this design feature (see Figure 12.3)
3 Get children into groups of three and ask them to come up with a fun name for their team. Then challenge them to design and make their balloon car, based on the designs shown in Figures 12.1 and 12.2. Older children may have other ideas and suggestions for their design
4 Once made, children test out their cars to try and make improvements, before racing against the other teams. Cars are raced one at a time in a time trial (you can do the 'best of three,' if time permits). Add the results to your racing series leader board

4–7 years – children use one of the designs shown. They make observations about how the car moves

7–9 years – children use one of the designs shown, but adapt it with their own ideas. They make observations and offer scientific suggestions about how the car moves

9–11 years – children use the designs to inspire their own ideas for a balloon car. They describe how the car moves, using terms such as *air pressure* and *energy*. They try out different designs to see which goes faster and adapt designs to make improvements

Key questions

- How does the car move?
- How could you make it go faster?

Helpful hints

- Note: when a balloon is blown up, the air pressure and stretched rubber inside the balloon create potential energy. When you let go of the balloon, the air is squeezed out of the balloon, converting the potential energy into kinetic energy

Figure 12.1 Balloon car

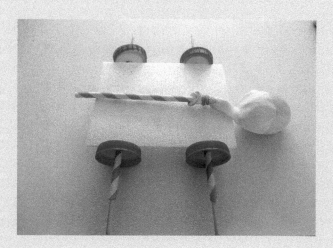

Figure 12.2 Balloon car

Figure 12.3 Freely rotating axels

Prep for next session (cotton reel car race)

Make a cotton reel car prior to the next session, making sure you forget to add in the washer!

Session two
Cotton reel car race

Following on from last time's balloon car time trial, this week children will be taking their design skills up a notch as they create a cotton reel car.

Resources needed

Cotton reel car made without the washer, cotton reels; spent matches or chopped skewers; elastic bands; pencils; flat washers; pencil alternatives: straws, nails, skewers; matchstick alternatives: paper clips, pipe cleaners

Activity

1   Ask children to remind you what powered their car the last time. Recap that the air inside the balloon shot out, resulting in the car being forced in the opposite direction. Show children Figure 12.4 and ask them how they think this car works

2   Explain that the cotton reel car is powered by the elastic band. Energy is added by twisting the pencil, which in turn twists the elastic band inside the car. When the car is ready to race, the elastic band is released. It unwinds very quickly, making the cotton reel rotate, and the car zooms away

3   Show children your example and ask why it doesn't work very well. Explain there is too much friction. Show children the making process (see Figures 12.5 and 12.6), and ask them where the washer should go (between the match and the cotton reel)

4   In their teams, children create a range of cotton reel cars with the aim of making them move as fast as they can. Children will need to problem solve like the pros to get their car moving fast enough to top the leader board! Once made, children test out their cars and make improvements before racing against other teams. Cars race in turn in a time trial, with results added to the leader board

4–7 years – children create cars and test them with and without washers. They make observations about how the cars move. They try out alternatives to the pencils

7–9 years – children create cars and test them with and without washers. They make observations and offer scientific suggestions about how the cars move. They try alternatives to the pencils and matchsticks

9–11 years – children create cars and suggest alternatives to the washer. They describe how the car moves and why the washer helps using terms such as *friction* and *energy*. They try out different designs to see which goes faster

Key questions

● How does the car move?
● How does the washer help?

Helpful hints

● Note: when the elastic band is wound up, it stores potential energy, which is then converted into kinetic energy when it is released and starts to untwist

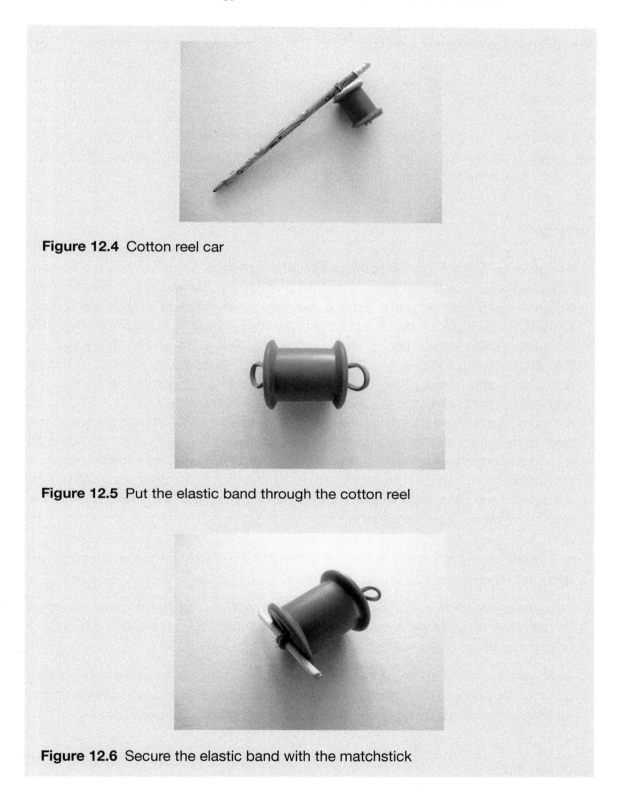

Figure 12.4 Cotton reel car

Figure 12.5 Put the elastic band through the cotton reel

Figure 12.6 Secure the elastic band with the matchstick

Prep for next session (power boat race)

Make sure that you have a water tray or trough for racing the boats created in the next session

Session three
Power boat race

Now that children own the roads with their car designs, they are going to move onto the water as they try out the same power moves to propel a boat onto the leader board. They will need to make some modifications, though, to make sure their boats don't sink.

Resources needed

Aluminium foil; foil trays; card; cardboard boxes; paper; empty water bottles; cotton reels; elastic bands; burnt/used matches; flat washers; duct tape; masking tape; sticky tape; lolly sticks; pencils; straws; corks; a water tray or piping

Activity

1   Ask children if they think the concept behind the balloon car and the cotton reel car would work for a boat as well as a car. Yes, but they would need to be adapted. They would need to use items that act like oars and would need to change the design. Children can still use a wound elastic band, but not necessarily in the same way. They would also need to think about how to ensure the balloon doesn't fill with water

2   Explain that today children are going to use both of these power sources to design and build boats to race. They will need to think carefully about the different shape and form of the vehicle, as well as the suitability of the materials

3   In their teams, children design at least one powered boat. They work through trial and error to determine that some materials (e.g. cardboard) don't work well in the water. If children struggle with ideas, show them Figures 12.7 and 12.8 for inspiration

4   Once made, children test out their boats to try and make improvements, before racing against the other teams. Boats are raced one at a time in a time trial. Add the results to your race series leader board

4–7 years – children create one boat and eliminate unsuitable materials through trial and error. They make simple modifications as issues arise

7–9 years – children create one boat and eliminate unsuitable materials based on an understanding of materials. They modify their boats as issues arise and consider how shape might affect speed

9–11 years – children create two boats and eliminate unsuitable materials based on an understanding of materials. They modify their boats to address issues and to make improvements. They create boat shapes that reduce water resistance

Key questions

● How does the boat move?
● How could you make it go faster?

Helpful hints

- Children may realise that the duct tape is better than the masking tape, as it stays on in water

Figure 12.7 Balloon boat

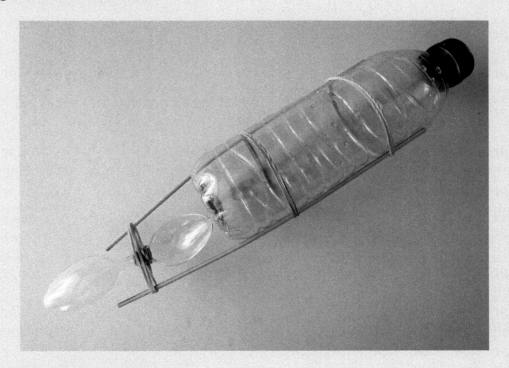

Figure 12.8 Elastic band boat

Prep for next session (soap boat race)

Check for any soap allergies for next session

Session four
Soap boat race

This week, children are going to try an alternative power source to the ones used so far. They will explore the power of surfactants to send their boats speeding across the water.

Resources needed

Water; rice cereal; washing-up liquid; thick card; scissors; PVA glue; liquid hand soap; hand cleaning gel; cotton buds; a water tray or piping

Activity

1 Ask children how they think they could use washing-up liquid to power a boat. Have a plate of water, and sprinkle some rice cereal onto it. Take a cotton bud of washing-up liquid and place it near the centre of the plate. The cereal should shoot out to the edge of the plate

2 Explain that the soap breaks the surface tension of the water, making water molecules pull away from the broken tension and taking the cereal with it. This kind of substance is called a surfactant. Ask children how this principle might be used to power a boat

3 In their teams, children make boats of varying sizes similar in design to Figure 12.9. They then test out their boats (see Figure 12.10) with four different surfactants (washing-up liquid, PVA glue; liquid hand soap; hand cleaning gel) to see which works best

4 Once made, children race their boats against the other teams. Do heats, building up to semifinals and a final. Add the results to your race series leader board

4–7 years – children test three possible surfactants and describe what they see. Children also try different amounts of each surfactant to see if it changes the performance

7–9 years – children test all possible surfactants and explain what is causing the movement. Children also try different amounts of each surfactant to see if it changes the performance

9–11 years – children test all possible surfactants and explain what is causing the movement using scientific terms such as *water tension* and *molecule*. Children try different amounts of each surfactant, as well as different boat sizes to see if these variables impact performance. Their investigation should show evidence of fair testing

Key questions

● What causes the boat to move?
● Which surfactant makes the boat go fastest?
● Do you think boat size and volume of surfactant affect the speed of the boat?

Helpful hints

● Note: a surfactant is a substance that breaks the surface tension of water

Figure 12.9 Boat shape

Figure 12.10 Soap-powered boat

Prep for next session (parachute slow race)

Ask children to bring in any Lego people they may have at home

Session five
Parachute slow race

Speed has been the order of the day up until now, but during this week's session, children are going to have to slow it down somewhat. Their challenge today is to create slow-falling parachutes. Slow and steady will win this race.

Resources needed

Plastic bin bags; string or wool; Lego people; scissors; sticky tape; yoghurt pots

Activity

1   Ask children what they think: to ensure a safe landing after falling or jumping from a great height, is it better to be travelling quickly or slowly? Note that gravity pulls things towards the ground, but that air resistance pushes up against a falling object, slowing it down. The larger the surface area of something, the greater the air resistance, and the slower the object will fall. Explain that today children are going to harness this air resistance and see if they can land a Lego person safely on the ground, having dropped it from a height, using a bin-bag parachute
2   Show children the bin bags and explain that they need to cut out shapes for their parachutes to see which makes the most effective (slowest-falling) parachute. Also encourage them to test the number and length of the pieces of string they attach to the parachute in order to secure their passenger's yoghurt pot seat (see Figure 12.11)
3   In their teams, children try out various shapes of parachute (circle, oval, square, rectangle, hexagon, etc.) and test different string configurations. Emphasise that testing needs to be logical and fair. Once they have finished testing and have a final design, teams race their parachutes against each other – last one to the ground wins

4–7 years – children test out two different shapes, and two string lengths. They stick to four strings on each parachute. Children make observations and offer an explanation for the movement of the parachute

7–9 years – children test out three different shapes and three string lengths. They stick to four strings on each parachute. Children make observations and offer an explanation for the movement of the parachute. They relate features of their parachute to its success (e.g. more air can be caught)

9–11 years – children test out three different shapes and three string lengths. They also test different numbers of strings. Children describe what they observe in scientific language using the terms *gravity*, *surface area* and *air resistance*. They identify those features of a parachute that contribute to its success

Key questions

● Why does the parachute move slowly?
● What difference does the size and shape of the parachute and the string length make?

Helpful hints

● Tie the string onto the parachute rather than taping it

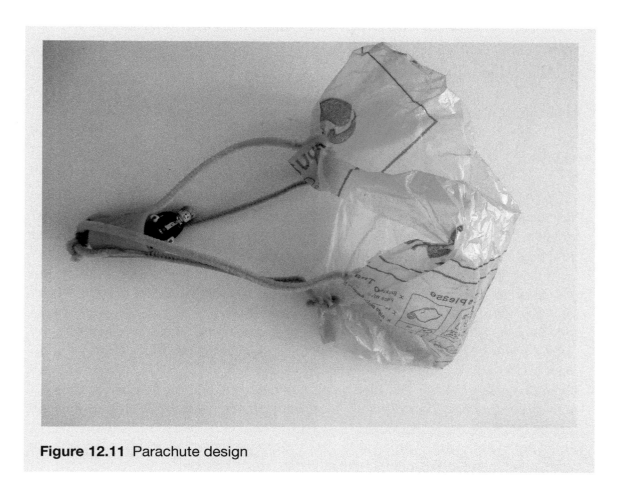

Figure 12.11 Parachute design

Prep for next session (flying saucers)

Source paper plates of varying sizes for the next session

Session six
Flying saucers

Children have raced on the roads, sped across water and drifted down to earth. Today, they are going to fly through the sky as they create the ultimate flying saucer.

Resources needed

Frisbee; paper plates (two sizes); sticky tape; scissors; felt tip pens

Activity

1 Give children a demonstration of your Frisbee. Throw it flat (correctly) at first, then try it vertically. Which way works best? Ask children why they think when thrown horizontally the Frisbee travels a long way. Explain that while the spin keeps it stable, lift and drag cause the Frisbee to glide through the air
2 Explain that children will work in their teams again today to design a flying saucer that can fly as far as possible. Start by joining two paper plates together to make a basic structure (see Figure 12.12). Children can then test designs with no hole, a small hole, or a large hole (see Figures 12.12–12.14), as well as trying different sized plates
3 Give children time to experiment, encouraging them to think of their own ideas about how to make their flying saucer travel further
4 Once they have finished testing and have chosen a final design, teams compete in a 'flying saucer flying competition' – furthest distance covered wins. Children score points to add to the leader board

4–7 years – children test out two different plate sizes, with and without a hole. Children describe what they see and offer an explanation for the movement of the flying saucer

7–9 years – children test out two different plate sizes, as well as two different sizes of holes. They describe what they see and offer an explanation for the movement of the flying saucer. They relate features of their flying saucer to its success

9–11 years – children test out two different plate sizes, as well as various hole sizes. Children describe what they see in scientific language using the terms *lift* and *air resistance*. They identify those features of a flying saucer that contribute to its success

Key questions

● Why does the flying saucer glide through the air?
● What difference does having a hole make? Does the size of the hole matter?

Helpful hints

● Note: the air above the flying saucer travels at a greater velocity than that beneath it, which creates different pressures, creating lift
● Note: spinning keeps the flying saucer stable as it glides

Figure 12.12 Flying saucer design

Figure 12.13 Flying saucer with a small hole

Figure 12.14 Flying saucer with a large hole

Prep for next time

Have a look through and decide which topic you will do next time – the introduction page
of each chapter will tell you what you need to prep